BOOK TWO

ROBINSON CRUSOE MARKING HIS POST.

(*See page 106.*)

NELSON'S
WEST INDIAN READERS

Book TWO

Compiled by J. O. Cutteridge

PREFATORY NOTE FOR TEACHERS

THE second book of the series has been prepared on the same plan as the first. Teachers are advised to read the Prefatory Note in Book I. on the aims of the series and the method of treatment to be followed.

It is again emphasized that the exercises lose their value unless the pupils *discover* the answers for themselves.

J. O. CUTTERIDGE.

CONTENTS

An Asterisk (*) indicates Poetry

1.	CORN	7
2.	THE MOROCOY'S ADVENTURE	10
3.	WATER-VAPOUR	14
4.	EAST INDIANS IN THE WEST INDIES	17
5.	*THE BEGGAR MAID	21
6.	RICE	23
7.	SEA TURTLES	27
8.	KEEP THE BODY CLEAN	31
9.	HOMES IN OTHER LANDS	34
10.	WRITING A LETTER	42
11.	*HOW TO WRITE A LETTER	45
12.	DEW AND RAIN	47
13.	ALICE IN WONDERLAND	50
14.	MAMMALS	57
15.	FRESH AIR	63
16.	SOME COMMON INSECTS	66
17.	SPONGE-FISHING	70
18.	*WYNKEN, BLYNKEN, AND NOD	74
19.	THE STORY OF COLUMBUS	78
20.	GRASSES	84
21.	A VOYAGE TO LONDON	88
22.	WINDS	96
23.	THE MONKEY AND THE ALLIGATOR	101

CONTENTS

24.	ROBINSON CRUSOE	105
25.	EXERCISE	113
26.	*THE MOCK TURTLE'S SONG	116
27.	FRUIT TREES	118
28.	A COUNTRY OF FORESTS	124
29.	A BRIDGE OF CROCODILES	128
30.	*LULLABY OF AN INFANT CHIEF	133
31.	PANDORA'S BOX	135
32.	BIRDS	143
33.	PICTURES AND STORIES	149

READING TESTS AND EXERCISES 153
*ADDITIONAL POETRY FOR READING AND
   RECITATION 165

Acknowledgements

The author and the publisher would also like to thank the following for permission to reproduce material:

Text Permissions

p173: reprinted by permission of The Literary Trustees of Walter de la Mare and The Society of Authors as their Representative.

Images

p20: EPA/Alamy; p22: 'For a moment they stood looking at each other - the barefoot beggar girl in her rags and the King in his jewelled crown', King Cophetua and the Beggar Maid (colour litho), Michael, Arthur C. (fl.1903-28) (after)/Private Collection/The Stapleton Collection/The Bridgeman Art Library; p25: David Pearson/Alamy; p55: Harry Rountree; p67: Amazon-Images/Alamy; p71: Alvis Uptis/Alamy; p75: S.B. Pearce; p79: Science and Society Picture Library; p92: Pf/Alamy; p93: Rolf Richardson/Robert Harding Picture Library/Corbis; p94: Look Die Bildgenteur der Fotografen GmbH/Alamy; p107: Classic Image/Alamy; p150: The Arab Tale-teller, 1833 (oil on canvas), Vernet, Emile Jean Horace (1789-1863)/© Wallace Collection, London, UK/The Bridgeman Art Library; p159: Ivy Close/Alamy.

Every effort has been made to trace the copyright holders but if any have been inadvertently overlooked the publisher will be pleased to make the necessary arrangements at the first opportunity.

LESSON 1

CORN

PERHAPS you can finish the nursery rhyme which begins like this:

> "Little Boy Blue, come blow up your horn,
> The sheep's in the meadow, the cow's in the corn."

Do you know why the cow was in the corn? If you read this lesson carefully you may be able to answer the question correctly.

Look at a corn plant and you will see that the stem is jointed, and that the leaves are long, flat, and broad. It is somewhat like sugar-cane, and belongs to the same family of plants.

Many roots may be seen coming out from the joints of the stem just above the ground. They grow downwards into the soil and help to hold the plant upright.

The top of the plant bears flowers which contain a kind of yellow powder called "pollen dust". Shake a plant gently and you will see some of it falling.

The ears of the corn grow out from the places where the leaves join the stem. There are silky tassels at the end of each ear of corn. These are also flowers. The yellow powder from the other flowers falls on these tassels, and causes the seeds to grow on the cobs.

Each cob has a number of thin coverings called husks or sheaths. These protect the young seeds and prevent the birds from eating them.

If you look at a ripe ear of corn you will see that the husks are white.

On removing the husks you will find that the seeds are either yellow, white, red, or black, and that they are fixed in regular rows on the cob. Sometimes seeds of different colours are seen on the same cob. Each cob is joined to the stem by means of a stalk.

The corn plant is very useful. The leaves, the sheaths or husks and the stalks serve as fodder for cattle. Paper can also be made from the husks and the stalks.

The miller grinds the corn into fine flour called corn-meal or corn-flour.

The baker knows that children are very fond of eating all the nice things made from corn, and so he makes corn-cakes, flakes, and lovely pop-corns for them. We also like the green corn when it is young, and corn roasted on the cob makes a tasty dish.

The farmer feeds his cattle, hogs, poultry, horses, and milking-cows on corn. Why? Because he knows that it is one of the richest foods in the world for these animals. Now try to answer the question in the second paragraph.

In many countries, the plant that we call corn is known as maize, and when the people of those lands speak of corn they mean wheat, oats, or barley.

Exercises

1. Take a good cob of corn and count the number of rows on it. Do the same with three more cobs. Have they all the same number of rows?

2. In what ways is corn like sugar-cane?
3. Give other words which mean the same as—husks, pollen dust, stalks, milking-cows, and fodder.
4. If a boy in England said "The cow's in the corn," what plant would the cow be eating?
5. Finish these sentences:
   >The cob is . . . . .
   >The husk . . . . .
   >Maize is . . . . .
   >Pollen dust . . . . .
   >Silky tassels are . . . . .

LESSON 2

THE MOROCOY'S* ADVENTURE

A CREOLE FOLK-TALE

ONCE upon a time the birds were all invited to a party by Mr. Gabilan, the chicken-hawk, at his house in "Cloudland", some distance above the earth. Now the morocoy was very friendly with the fowls, ducks, and pigeons who lived near him.

As morocoys also lay eggs, he thought he was a kind of cousin to them, and he was very

---

* Morocoy is Creole for tortoise.

much upset because he had not been invited too.

Those birds agreed that as the morocoy lays eggs very like those of a fowl, they might allow him to go with them. But how was he to get up to Mr. Gabilan's house in the sky when he had no wings?

Wishing to please him, however, as he was a good neighbour, they each lent him a feather, to enable him to fly like a bird so that he could reach the house. You must remember that in those days he was not such an ugly lumpy thing as he is now.

CHICKEN-HAWK.

Miss Peahen, who was dressed in fine robes, just like those now worn only by Mr. Peacock, was asked to sing for the company, and she did so. Now Mr. Morocoy, like the foolish fellow he was, said that her dress was lovely, but that her voice was awful.

Every one knows that the voice of a peacock is not very sweet, but if the morocoy had been thoughtful he would have known that it is not always wise to say what one thinks.

Miss Peahen was the favourite of all the young men-birds, and when they heard his remarks they became angry. The party broke up, and the birds took back their feathers from the tortoise, who was left in a sad plight as he was now unable to return to the earth.

He was very sorry for what he had said, and Mrs. Spider, who happened to be there, took pity on him, and offered to spin him a line by means of which he could get back to Mother Earth.

The morocoy was rather doubtful if the silken cord of the spider could bear his weight, but as that was the only chance for him he started on his journey downwards.

Alas! when about two hundred feet from the earth, the thin cord gave way, and he fell with such force to the ground that every bone in his body was broken.

He had to be wrapped in so many bandages that they stuck to him and could not be removed.

So he remains as if he were in splints until this day—an ugly misshapen creature, with small badly formed legs.

He is a warning to other people not to be too free with their tongues when speaking of their betters.

Exercises

1. Give another name for the chicken-hawk.
2. In what way is the morocoy like a bird?
3. How did the morocoy get to the party?
4. How did he return?
5. Why do you think the peahen was the favourite of all the men-birds?
6. Does the peacock sing sweetly? How do you know?
7. What happened when the cord broke?
8. What lesson can you learn from this story?

LESSON 3

WATER-VAPOUR

When people wash their clothes they often put them on the ground to dry. When the clothes are dry we can no longer see or feel the water that was in them; it has disappeared. Where has it gone to?

If water is poured on dry sand, the sand swallows it up or *absorbs* it; it disappears. But we can see that the sand is wet, because its colour is different, and we can feel that it is wet.

When our clothes dry in the air, the air absorbs the water that is in them. We cannot see this water in the air, nor can we feel it, because it is now thin like air. But although we cannot see or feel it, there is always some water in the air, sometimes more, sometimes less.

Wet clothes dry very quickly when the sun is shining brightly, and when they are spread out on the warm sand or on a beach. They dry more slowly when the sky is cloudy, or at night. They dry quickly, also, when they are hung before a fire. We see, therefore, that heat makes them dry quickly.

We also know that in the hot weather in the dry season the water in tanks and pools quickly becomes less. If we look carefully, we can see the water sinking lower from day to day. This is because it is being absorbed by the air.

We know, too, that water spilt on a stone floor in a house soon dries up. It also is absorbed by the air. The air is always absorbing water, and the hotter it is the more it absorbs.

Now, in order that the air may absorb water, the water must become thin like air. Water in this state is called water-vapour.

When water is boiled, it turns very rapidly into water-vapour. Bubbles keep coming up from the bottom of the vessel in which it is boiled. These are bubbles of water-vapour, not bubbles of air.

Even when water is not boiling, it is always slowly turning into water-vapour; but this vapour comes from the top of the water, and so we see no bubbles. When water turns quietly into invisible vapour in this way, it is said to *evaporate.*

Now remember that on the earth there is three times as much water as land, and that the air is always absorbing water-vapour from this water. We know, therefore, that the air must be full of water-vapour although we cannot see it.

EXERCISES

1. When clothes are dried, where does the water go?
2. Why cannot we see or feel the water in the air?
3. When do wet clothes dry quickly?
4. What makes things dry quickly?
5. When does water in tanks and pools quickly become less?
6. What is water-vapour?
7. What makes the bubbles in boiling water?
8. When does water evaporate?
9. How many times more sea than land is there on the earth?

LESSON 4

EAST INDIANS IN THE WEST INDIES

If Columbus could wake up and come again to the West Indies* he might easily think he had reached India, for he would see many East Indians here now.

In our First Book we read that the parents or grandparents of the East Indian boys and girls of our colonies came from India. It is not strange, therefore, to see many of them doing the same kind of work, wearing the same kind of clothes, and eating the same kind of food as the people of India.

The East Indians came to work in the sugar-cane fields of the West Indies and Guyana. They worked hard on the fields, and those who were thrifty saved as much money as they could. Many of them are now sugar-cane farmers, owners of cocoa and coconut estates, and shopkeepers. Some are doctors, lawyers, and ministers or clergymen.

* See Lesson 19.

Much rice is grown in India, and it is one of their crops here also. They are the only people engaged in rice-planting in the lagoon lands of the West Indies, Belize and Guyana.

A great many of them are gardeners. They grow all kinds of vegetables for the market. They also raise a very large quantity of poultry, and keep cows from which they get milk to sell.

The rich East Indians live in fine houses, and wear costly dresses and jewels. They ride about in motor-cars as there are no elephants here for them to ride.

The poor East Indians live in huts built of mud, and roofed with cane-trash, rice-stalks, water-grass, or carat leaves. How many of you know what an ajoupa is?

Most East Indian women in the West Indies wear long skirts, bodices with short sleeves, and orhnis. The sari is seldom worn except for ceremonies, because much of their time is spent in field-work.

The East Indian jeweller makes all kinds of pretty jewels of gold, silver, and precious stones. The women wear these on their arms, nose, and

LESSON 4

THINGS MADE OF GOLD AND SILVER BY EAST INDIANS.

ears, around their necks and ankles, and on their fingers and toes.

There are pretty Hindu and Muslim temples in many parts of the West Indies where the East Indians of those faiths go to worship.

INDIAN HORSE PROCESSION.

The boys do not always follow the same trade or calling as their parents and grandparents, as is the custom in India. They often like to do other things, and may be seen busily engaged in various kinds of skilled labour.

The East Indians and West Indians are very kind and friendly towards one another. They live quite happily together, and are all loyal to their Country.

Exercises

1. Why are East Indians good rice-planters?
2. Make a list of all the occupations of East Indians given in this lesson.
3. Write out a list of all the birds which we call poultry.
4. How many sentences are there in this lesson? How many paragraphs? How many questions?
5. If you went to India what would you expect to see the people wearing and doing?

LESSON 5

THE BEGGAR MAID

Introduction.—A certain African king named Cophetua would not marry, although his nobles begged him to do so. One day, however, as he was sitting in state, a beautiful beggar maid passed by. He fell in love with her, and soon after married her. Here is a poem about this.

Her arms across her breast she laid;
   She was more fair than words can say:
Barefooted came the beggar maid
   Before the king Cophetua.
In robe and crown the king stept* down,
   To meet and greet her on the way:

---

* In prose, *stepped*.

"It is no wonder" said the lords;
  "She is more beautiful than day."

As shines the moon in clouded skies,
  She in her poor attire was seen:
One praised her ankles, one her eyes,
  One her dark hair and lovesome mien.
So sweet a face, such angel grace,
  In all that land had never been:
Cophetua sware* a royal oath:
  "This beggar maid shall be my queen!"
                        TENNYSON.

* In prose, *swore*.

Exercises

1. Where did King Cophetua live?
2. What did his nobles beg him to do?
3. Who passed by when he was sitting in state?
4. What did the king do?
5. Was the beggar maid proud?
6. How do you know that she was not?
7. Was she beautifully dressed?
8. What does the poem say about her clothes?
9. What was her hair like?
10. What was Cophetua's royal oath?
11. Write out all the words which rhyme in the poem.

LESSON 6

RICE

The rice which we buy in the shops has been cleaned and polished for us. Before it was cleaned the little grains were hidden in close-fitting jackets called husks. When the grains are in their beautiful white, yellow, brown, red, or black husks they are called paddy.

Paddy plants are grown in the lagoon lands of many of the West Indian islands, Belize, and

Guyana. They are also grown in other warm countries such as India, Burma, and China.

The soil must be well forked or ploughed before the seeds are sown, and the plants need a great deal of water while they are growing.

RICE.

The lands are therefore divided into plots, around which mounds of earth are raised to keep in the water.

The paddy is sown in nurseries, and then transplanted into the larger fields. Soon afterwards each plant sends up a large number of shoots. The roots look like bundles of very fine threads. You learned in Book I. that it belongs to the grass family.

The stem and leaves are mostly green in colour, but sometimes they are red or purple. The leaves are thin and long, and the stem is hollow and jointed.

Each stem or shoot bears an ear which is very much branched, as you can see in the picture on page 24. Every little branch bears a grain of paddy. Sometimes a single stalk has more than five hundred grains, so that a plant with ten stalks may yield as many as five thousand grains.

When the grains are ripe, the stalks are cut down and threshed. The paddy is then put into bags and carried to the barns, where it is dried in the sun.

A RICE FIELD.

Some people keep large quantities of paddy in their houses for the use of their families. They remove the husks from the grains by pounding them in wooden mortars.

The paddy which they do not need is carried to the mills, where the husks are removed and the grains cleaned and polished by machinery. These grains are then known as rice. It is put into bags, either to be sold at home or sent away to other countries.

The paddy plant is very useful, even after the ears have been removed. People cover their houses and sheds with the stalks. The stalks are also used for making paper.

Three different kinds of rice are Patna rice, Siam rice, and Demerara rice. They get their names from the places where the paddy was grown. There is also hill rice or mountain rice, which is grown in the West Indies.

Rice is a starchy food. It can be boiled and eaten with vegetables, meat, or fish. It can also be ground into fine flour called rice-flour, and made into puddings and cakes.

Exercises

1. In what countries is rice grown?
2. Why do you think that rice grows best on flat lands?

3. How many colours are mentioned in this lesson? Write them all down.
4. What is the difference between rice and paddy?

LESSON 7

SEA TURTLES

If you have ever been to the coast, you may have been lucky enough to see a sea turtle. There are many different kinds found throughout the West Indies, including the hawk's bill and the green turtle. They feed in the shallow waters near the coasts and at certain times the females come ashore to lay eggs on a beach.

The female sea turtle always returns to lay her own eggs on the very same beach where she hatched. She digs a hole for the eggs then covers them over with sand. She will normally lay between two and six times during a year and each time she produces between eighty and two hundred eggs. The warm sand helps the baby turtles to develop inside the eggs. Once hatched, the small turtles dig their way to the surface and then crawl to the sea. Many are caught by predators during their scramble between the nest and the water.

Once in the water the hatchlings find feeding grounds, often in seagrass beds or around coral reefs. They spend most of their life at sea, sometimes travelling for thousands of kilometres. It can take anywhere between twelve and forty years for a turtle to become a mature adult and many scientists estimate that only one turtle survives to this stage from every thousand eggs laid.

Hundreds of years ago, there were millions of sea turtles in the waters of the Caribbean Sea. Today, the number of these creatures is much smaller and most species are threatened with extinction, which means that they could die out completely and disappear forever. What has happened to affect the populations of sea turtles so badly?

For many centuries, turtles were caught for food and for their shells, which could be made into many different items. The number of people living in the Caribbean increased and turtle products were traded with other countries. More turtles were caught, sometimes to a point where local breeding populations were wiped out.

In recent times, the natural environments where the turtles live have all suffered. Their feeding grounds have been polluted by oil-spills and by chemicals and fertilizers running off the land. Their nesting beaches are being damaged and sometimes females do not want to come on the beach to nest because of too much human activity. Turtles are also trapped in fishing nets and can die if they eat plastic rubbish in the sea.

Today, sea turtles are protected by special laws. Many organisations around the Caribbean work to look after the remaining sea turtles and their natural habitats and to teach everyone how to do the same. If enough is done then people in the future will be able to enjoy seeing these wonderful, mysterious creatures.

Exercises

1. The female turtle can return to the beach where she was born because of a natural skill called a 'homing instinct'. Do you know of any other birds or animals that have this?
2. What are two of the sea turtles natural feeding areas?
3. Why were turtles hunted in the past?
4. What are two threats to the turtles' natural habitats?
5. How long does it take for a turtle to become a mature adult?
6. 'Turtle-watching', where people are able to witness female turtles nesting, is popular with tourists. Why do you think people would enjoy this activity?

LESSON 8

KEEP THE BODY CLEAN

THE first lesson on health that I have to learn is this: *I must keep my body clean.* At school a boy will sometimes be seen with dirty hands or a dirty face. This should never be. It is a disgrace to the boy and a disgrace to his school.

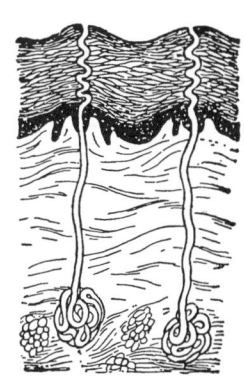

SECTION THROUGH SKIN (MUCH ENLARGED).

We should never be seen with dirty hands, dirty nails, or a dirty face. All should be kept clean and tidy. But that is not enough. The parts of the body that are covered with clothes also need to be washed.

Most of the dirt that gathers on the body comes not from the outside but from the inside of the body. The skin is full of little pores. These are the mouths of short pipes, which run from the flesh out through the skin. You can see them in this picture, which shows a little piece of the skin, cut through from the inside to the outside, and made very much larger. These pores are like tiny windows in the walls of our house, the body.

When we open a window, it lets in fresh air and lets out foul air. This is just what the pores do. They breathe in fresh air like little lungs, and they allow bad air and moisture to get out. If the skin is not kept clean by frequent washing, the little pores cannot do their work. In this way the health is injured.

We perspire freely when we run a race or play football or cricket. When we cool down, some of the perspiration dries on the skin, and there it remains till it is washed away.

If the skin is kept clean, the pores do their work day and night. They are outlets for what would be harmful to the body. But nothing can pass through them if they are choked up with dirt. So we must keep the skin clean, or the health is sure to suffer.

Once upon a time a king was coming to visit a certain town, and the people went out to meet him, dressed in many kinds of gay and curious dresses so as to amuse their great visitor. They took a little boy and covered his skin all over with thin leaves of gold, so that he might look like a golden boy.

No doubt he looked very pretty, but he turned ill and died before the gilding could be removed. All the pores of his skin were closed up by the gold, and it soon caused his death.

Water is useful for a great many purposes. It is good to drink, and it is good to wash with. Soap is also cheap. Water and soap are all that is needed to keep the skin clean and ready for its work.

In Holland there is a village which is said to be the cleanest in the world. The houses inside and outside, the streets and everything about the place, are kept in a state of spotless cleanliness.

Women may be seen scrubbing the outsides of their houses and squirting water on the windows to keep them clean. We should be like these Dutch people, in keeping that wonderful house, the body, clean. It is only by often washing the whole body that we can keep in good health.

Exercises

Fill in the blanks:
1. Dutch people live in ____.
2. The moisture on the skin is sometimes called sweat. ____ is the proper name for it.
3. We should bathe the ____ of our bodies.
4. The little ____ are called pores.

LESSON 9

HOMES IN OTHER LANDS

WOULD you like to come with me across the wide ocean to see the homes of boys and girls in other countries? Here is a large steamer in the harbour which will take us away from the West Indies.

For many days we sail on and on towards the north until we come to the very cold countries. There are no cane-fields, cocoa-trees, or coconut palms to be seen now, nor are there any green fields and savannahs. All around the ground is white, as this is the land of snow and ice.

What are those round lumps like basins turned upside down? They are the houses in which the Eskimo children live. Can you see the long tunnel through which they crawl when they go in and out? Touch the walls and you will find they feel very cold, for they are made of blocks of snow and ice.

ESKIMO SNOW HOUSES.

Such houses would not last long in the West Indies as the heat of the sun would melt them, but in the cold lands they form very cosy homes in winter, and keep out the keen winds.

The boys and girls are playing on the ice with a sledge, or in their boats made of skins. Some of them are coming home with their fathers, who have been hunting the seals and polar bears. They get their food and clothing as well as the oil for their lamps from these animals. See how their bodies are closely covered with clothes made of skin or fur. We should be very hot in such garments, but they could not do without them.

Let us leave the cold lands and sail away south to another country. Here we find it is very hot and dry. Rain hardly ever falls, and nothing seems to grow in this big sea of sand or desert.

The people are called Arabs. You can see some of them in the picture on page 38. They wear long, loose white clothes, to keep off the heat of the sun. A party of them has just come to the end of their journey. A tent has been set up covered with striped cloth made of goat's hair.

Perhaps you have heard of the "ship of the desert". This is a name which is often given to the camel, because it is only on camels that men can cross the great sea of sand. Here and there are pleasant green places where water is found and a few palm-trees are growing. Such a place is called an oasis. A little school is often found there.

When we build our houses, we want them to last for some time, and they are often big and heavy. The Arabs are always moving about, and so they must have houses which can be taken down quickly and carried on the backs of their camels.

RED INDIAN WIGWAMS.

We will now go to another part of the world to see some more people who live in tents. The Red Indians of North America are hunters, and move about from place to place in search of the animals they kill for food. Their houses are

ARAB CAMP IN THE DESERT.

therefore made of a few poles covered with skins, and are called wigwams. Horses drag the tent-poles along when they move to a new hunting-ground.

In the wide grassy plains in Asia lives another race of people called the Kirghis. They are not hunters, like the Red Indians, but shepherds, and they have great herds of sheep, cattle, goats, and horses. The animals eat up the thin grass very quickly, and so these people also are always moving about from place to place. Their houses are also tents, but they have upright sides and a roof, as you can see in the picture.

KIRGHIS TENTS.

Houses are mostly built on the ground, but there are people who live in the branches of trees, just like birds in their nests. These are forest dwellers, and their houses must be safe from the wild animals and from any people who would do them harm.

Another strange place for a home is in the middle of a lake or river. Strong posts are fixed so that they stand up out of the water, and on these the houses are built. As a rule the people who build such houses are fishermen.

In your geography lessons your teacher will tell you all about the homes of boys and girls in many other countries, such as the pygmies' huts in the forests, the bamboo houses in Japan, the Swiss huts on the mountain sides, and even about people who live in boats.

TREE DWELLINGS.

At first it may seem to us that the houses of all those people are funny houses because they are not like ours. We see, however, that they are very wise in making their homes to suit the countries in which they live. Their clothes, their food, and the work they do, are all different from ours, but there are reasons for all this. If those people came to the West Indies, our homes and our ways of living would seem just as strange to them.

Exercises

1. Draw the houses of the Eskimo, the Arab, the Red Indian, the Kirghis, and the tree-dweller.
2. Try to make a model of each of the houses given in the lesson.
3. Finish these sentences:

    The Eskimo makes his house of snow and ice *because* . . . . .

    The Arab lives in a tent *because* . . . . .

    The Kirghis move about *because* . . . . .

    The wigwam is made of poles and skins *because* . . . . .

    The tree-dweller builds his house high up *because* . . . . .

    The camel has flat feet *because* . . . .

LESSON 10

WRITING A LETTER

ONE day the letter-carrier came to a school. He brought two letters for the headmaster and one for one of the boys. The boy took his letter and looked at the address.

He read this, but he did not know from whom the letter came. The master said, "Open your letter, Charles. You cannot tell who sent it by looking at the outside."

Charles opened the envelope and took out his letter. It was written in English, so he read it easily. It was from his brother Harry, who was a clerk in the Warden's office in a town about twenty miles away.

In it Harry told Charles that he was well, and that he hoped soon to be promoted. He also said that the head clerk was kind to him, and that the Warden was satisfied with his work.

Charles was very much pleased with his letter, and he said to the master, "Please, sir, may I read my letter to the other boys?

It is from my brother Harry;" and the master told him to read it aloud.

When he had finished, the master said, "It is a very good letter. Your brother learned to write letters in this school; and it is time for you all to learn how to write a letter. You may each write one now to any one you please." He then asked each boy whom he would like to write to, and when each had answered, he said:

"I will now tell you how to write a letter. Each take a sheet of paper. In the top right-hand corner write, 'Government School' and below it 'Bridgetown.' Below this write the date—'1st April 1960.' Below the date and on the left-hand side of the page write 'Dear—,' putting the name of the person to whom you are writing."

The master wrote this on the blackboard for them to copy:

Government School,
Bridgetown,
1st April 1960.

Dear—

The master then said, "Having made a beginning, you can now write what you like in your letters. When you have finished that, you must write, 'I remain' and then, in a separate line, if the letter is to a relative, 'your affectionate son,' or 'brother,' or 'nephew,' or 'cousin'; if it is to a friend, 'your affectionate friend'; and then sign your names in the last line."

He then wrote on the blackboard:

I remain,
  Your affectionate son,

The boys all wrote the place and date and "Dear—," and then sat looking at the paper and biting their pens. They could not think what to write.

The master soon saw this, and said, "You do not know what to say. Dry with your blotting-paper what you have written, and put it into your desks. Tomorrow we will read a poem about writing a letter, and then you shall try again to write one."

Note to Teacher.—Use the address of your own school in lieu of the one given.

Exercises

1. What must you write at the top right-hand corner of your letter?
2. What must you write just below this?
3. Where must you write the date?
4. What do you write on the left-hand side of the page?
5. What do you write at the end of the letter?
6. What do you do with your blotting-paper?
7. Try to write a letter to one of your relatives.

LESSON 11

HOW TO WRITE A LETTER

Maria intended a letter to write,
But could not begin (as she thought) to indite;
So went to her mother with pencil and slate
Containing "Dear Sister," and also a date.

"With nothing to say, my dear girl, do not think
Of wasting your time over paper and ink;
But certainly this is an excellent way,
To try with your slate to find something to say.

"I will give you a rule", said her mother. "My dear,
Just think for a moment your sister is here,
And what would you tell her? Consider, and then,
Though silent your tongue, you can speak with your pen."

ELIZABETH TURNER.

Exercises

1. Who was Maria?
2. To whom did she intend to write?
3. On what was she going to write her letter?
4. Where did she write the date?
5. Where did she write "Dear Sister"?
6. Why is it a good way to write a letter first on a slate?
7. What else could you write on first?
8. Why could not Maria write her letter?
9. What rule did her mother give her?
10. What do you generally speak with?
11. What can you speak with when your tongue is silent?

LESSON 12

DEW AND RAIN

How beautiful the dew looks on the grass in the early morning! How does it come there? It is only water-vapour that has changed into drops of water again during the night.

We have seen that heat makes water evaporate. During the day, while the air is warmed by the sun, it absorbs water-vapour from the sea, and from every tank and river.

During the night, when the sun no longer shines, the air and the earth become cool again, and some of this water-vapour very gradually turns back into water, and we see it everywhere in the form of dewdrops.

Heat makes water turn into water-vapour, or *evaporate;* cold turns water-vapour into water again, or *condenses* it.

If you look up into the sky you will generally see clouds. In fine weather they look white and are high up; in wet weather, or when rain is coming, they are darker and nearer the earth. What are clouds?

When water is boiling you see steam. If you look carefully at the boiling water you do not see the steam close to the water, but only at a little distance above it. Why is this?

When the water is boiling much water-vapour rises from it. This hot water-vapour is invisible, but as it rises into the colder air above the vessel it begins to turn into water again, and then it becomes visible, and we see it as steam. Steam is really made up of very small drops of water. We might call it "water dust."

The clouds which you see in the sky are like steam. They are water-vapour turning back into water. If the air in which they are floating becomes colder, they turn into larger and heavier drops of water, and then fall as rain.

Exercises

1. When do we see the dew on the flowers?
2. What is dew?
3. Why is it formed during the night?
4. What are clouds like in fine weather?
5. What are clouds like when rain is coming?
6. What condenses water-vapour?
7. Why cannot you see steam close to boiling water?
8. When do the clouds fall as rain?

LESSON 13

ALICE IN WONDERLAND

ONE summer day a little girl named Alice fell asleep in the garden, and had a very strange dream. She saw in her dream a dear little White Rabbit with pink eyes. He wore a brown coat and a blue vest, and was holding his watch in one hand and a butterfly net in the other.

"Oh dear! oh dear! I shall be too late," he said to himself, as he moved away very fast on his hind feet. Alice was filled with wonder at the sight, and rose up to go after him.

In a moment the White Rabbit popped down a rabbit hole. Alice went after him, and found herself in a very dark place. All at once she found herself falling down, down, down into what seemed to be a very deep well. She thought she would never stop again, but at last she settled with a thump upon a pile of sticks and dry leaves. She was not hurt, and began at once to look about her. Then she saw the White Rabbit again, and jumped up to follow him. But he soon turned a corner and went out of sight.

Alice now looked around, and found that she was in a long room lit by lamps which hung near the roof. There were doors all round the walls, but when she tried to open them she found that they were all locked.

Not far from her stood a small table made of glass, and upon this table lay a golden key. Alice took up the key and tried to open the doors in the walls, one after the other. But the key would not fit any of the locks. Then she saw a door which was almost covered by a curtain. She tried the key in that door, and found that she could turn the lock.

Then she opened the door, and saw a long passage which led to a lovely garden. But the passage was only high enough for a rabbit to go through. Alice felt very sad, and put the key back on the table. She now saw a small bottle on the table. It had a slip of paper tied to the neck, on which were the words, "DRINK ME." Alice took out the cork and drank all that was in the bottle. At once she began to grow smaller and smaller and smaller, until she was only about ten inches high.

She was now of the right size to go down the passage. So she went back for the key. But she was now too small to reach up to the table, "What shall I do now?" she said.

All at once she saw a box under the glass table. She opened it, and found a cake on which were the words, "EAT ME." This she did, and at once began to grow taller and taller, until she was more than nine feet high.

She could now reach the key, but when she opened the door she could not go down the passage. So she sat down and cried until there was a pool of tears all round her.

After a time the White Rabbit came by, with a pair of white gloves in one hand and a fan in the other.

"If you please, sir," said Alice; but she said no more, for the White Rabbit got such a fright that he dropped the fan and the gloves and ran away. Alice picked up the fan and began to fan herself.

As she did so she found that she was growing smaller again. Smaller and smaller she grew, until she feared she would grow into nothing. But when she threw away the fan she stopped.

She was now small enough to go down the passage, but as she looked round for the key she fell into a pool of water. This was the pool of tears that she had made. As she swam about in it, she met a dear little mouse who was also swimming. "Let us get to shore" he said.

It was time they did, for the pool was now full of animals. There were a Duck and a Turkey, a Parrot and an Eagle, and many other strange creatures. All were very wet and very cross when they got to shore.

"The best way to get dry," said the Turkey, "is to have a race."

So they all stood in a ring. Then they started and ran about where they liked for half an hour. At last the Parrot cried, "The race is over. Who has won?"—"Who has won?" they cried in chorus.

"We have all won," said the Eagle, after thinking for a long time, "so we must all have prizes."

"SHE MET A DEAR LITTLE MOUSE."

(*Page 54.*)

"But who is to give the prizes?" they all asked.

"Why, *she,* of course," said the Turkey, pointing to Alice; and the whole party crowded round her, calling out, "Prizes! prizes!"

Alice had no idea what to do, but she felt in her pocket and found a box of sweets. There was just one for each of them, but none for herself.

"What else have you got?" asked the Duck.

"A thimble," said Alice.

"Then I will give you that as your prize," said the Duck. Alice thought this very odd; but as everything was odd down there, she bowed as she took her prize, and tried not to laugh.

Would you like to hear more of the things that Alice did? You can find them in the book from which this lesson was taken.

Lewis Carroll.
(*Adapted from "Alice in Wonderland"*)

Exercises

Fill in the blanks:
1. The rabbit had —— eyes, a —— coat, a —— vest, and held a —— in his hand.
2. Alice found herself in —— —— ——.
3. She unlocked the —— and saw a ——.
4. After she —— the liquid she grew less and less, but when she —— the —— she began to grow taller and taller.
5. She was afraid she would grow into —— so she ——.
6. Alice had a —— for her prize.

LESSON 14

MAMMALS

In Book I. you read of some of our animal friends such as the cow, goat, horse, mule, ass, sheep, cat, and dog. Another which could be added to this list is the pig. These are all called domestic or tame animals.

There is another way in which they are all alike, and that is, they all suckle their young. Animals which do this are said to belong to the same class, and are called *mammals*. You know that hens do not suckle their chicks, nor do frogs feed the little tadpoles in that way. These animals belong to other classes.

Now we will learn something of the wild mammals which are found in the West Indies and on the Main. All those given in this lesson suckle their young, whether they live on land or in the sea, or fly in the air.

Monkeys are a very interesting race. The red howling monkey (*macaque-rouge*) has a hollow bone in its throat which helps it to make a great noise. It is heard chiefly at dawn and sunset, and before rain. A smaller monkey is the matchin; those found in Trinidad are light-coloured, but they are dark-coloured on the Main.

In Grenada, St. Kitts, Barbados, and other islands there are the descendants of some African monkeys which had been brought here and had escaped many years ago. These, of course, were Old World monkeys, and they differ from the native or New World monkeys in several ways. They have cheek pouches in which to store their food, and their tails are of no use for holding on to anything. No New World monkeys have cheek pouches, and many of them have tails which serve as a fifth hand.

It seems strange to think that there is a mammal which can fly. This is the bat, which is called a "hand-winged" animal. Look at the picture and you can perhaps see why it is given this name. It has no wings, but its fore-feet, or "hands," have webs of skin which serve the same purpose.

Bats go abroad at dusk and rest by day, when they hang head downwards by their claws. Some are useful as insect eaters, others devour small fish, some eat fruit, and one, the vampire, sucks the blood of animals.

Animals which have sharp-edged teeth, and can gnaw or bite through hard substances, are called rodents. Common rats and mice first came from Europe, but many of those which live in the trees are native. You may have seen the active little squirrel with its bushy tail, springing from branch to branch in the trees. The porcupine also lives in high trees. It has a tail which it uses to secure a firm hold in its lofty home.

The agouti* and the paca or lappe* are useful rodents, as their flesh is very good to eat. On the Main there is an animal of this class as large as a sheep.

All through South America there are large cat-like animals. These are the jaguar, the ocelot, and the puma, and they kill deer and cattle. A smaller one, which is found also in some of the islands, is the tiger-cat. It is spotted somewhat like the jaguar.

You read of the mongoose in Book I. The tayra or wood dog is somewhat like it, but much larger. It can climb well, but the mongoose only climbs a little.

The raccoon (*chien-mangue*) is a brown animal with a brown and white ringed tail. It lives in swamps and eats crabs, and has the habit of washing its food. The otter is a fish-eater, but it is seldom seen.

The largest animal we have in these parts is the manatee or sea-cow. It is a big clumsy creature, eight feet long, and resembles a seal, but it has no hind limbs. It lives in the water and feeds on water-plants.

---

* In Belize the agouti is known as the Indian rabbit, and the lappe as the gibnut.

SOME WEST INDIAN MAMMALS.

There are several kinds of manicou or opossum, which range in size from that of a mouse to a small cat. They carry their many young on their backs.

Other mammals are the wild pig or quenk (a small hairy beast), the deer, and the ant-eater. We must not forget the whale, which sometimes visits our waters. Although it lives entirely in the sea it is a mammal, and has to rise to the surface to breathe. Occasionally one is washed ashore on the coast.

[*Note for Teacher.*—Creole French (patois) names are given in brackets. These should be used in countries where patois is spoken. See also Lesson 32.]

Exercises

1. Write out the names of all the mammals given in this lesson. How many are there? How many have you seen? What mammals have you seen that are not named?
2. Give all the words which mean *classes* of animals.
3. Finish these sentences:

    Domestic animals are . . . . .
    The African monkeys have . . . . .
    At 6 a.m. we heard . . . . .
    The jaguar . . . . .
    The sea-cow . . . . .
    The young manicou . . . . .

LESSON 15

FRESH AIR

THE second health lesson I have to learn is this—*I must breathe fresh air.* If a man cannot get air to breathe, he will die in a few seconds. But that is not all: if the air he breathes is not pure air it is of no use, and it may soon poison him.

Why do we need to breathe at all? Because the air contains a gas called oxygen, and a constant supply of this gas must be taken into the blood, or else we cannot remain in good health. When we breathe, the air passes through the nostrils, down into the lungs, and there it meets with the blood, which also flows through the lungs.

When passing through the lungs the blood runs through very small thin tubes, so thin that the oxygen of the air passes freely through them to the blood; but they are strong enough to keep the blood in its proper place. And as the oxygen gas passes inwards to the blood, another gas, which has to be got rid of, passes outwards from the blood, and is breathed out into the air.

Thus the air we breathe out is different from the air we breathe in. It has lost the gas which is necessary for our life and health, and it contains a gas which is hurtful to us. To breathe this air over again would be useless, as it contains too little oxygen, and would also be hurtful, as it contains a gas which has already been thrown off by the body.

If I live in a room that does not get fresh air, the air in it will soon become close and bad, because every time I breathe I take some of the oxygen out of it.

If a lighted candle is put under a glass bell so that no air can get in, it soon burns up all the oxygen, and then it goes out. If a small animal, such as a bird or a rabbit, is put under a similar bell, it uses up all the oxygen, and the rest of the air is of no use to it. In a few minutes it becomes faint; it is unable to stand up, and unless it gets fresh air, it will soon die.

Once, in a storm, the captain of a ship made all the passengers go down below. There they were crowded into a small cabin, with only one small window, or porthole, to let in fresh air. All night long the ship plunged deep into the waves, and the port-hole had to be firmly closed, so that no air could get in.

The passengers struggled and cried for help, but in the storm their cries were not heard on deck, where the captain and his men were battling with the storm. In the morning the storm was past, but when the cabin was opened two of the passengers were found dead. The bad air had poisoned them.

You may also have heard the story of the Black Hole of Calcutta, where a hundred and forty-six English prisoners were shut up in a small cell. They could not get enough air to breathe, and in the morning a hundred and twenty-three of them were found dead.

Exercises

Fill in the blanks:
1. We breathe in —— air, but we breathe out —— air.
2. The part of the air we need is called ——.
3. Windows, ——, and —— are opened to let in fresh air.
4. The passengers —— because they had been —— by the —— air.
5. —— of the prisoners were alive the —— morning.

LESSON 16

SOME COMMON INSECTS

In Book I. you learned how to know an insect when you see one, and also that there are very large numbers of insects. Many years ago a quarter of a million kinds were known, and in one island of the West Indies alone one hundred and forty-eight different sorts of ants have been found.

We will now read something of the life and habits of ants, bees, mosquitoes, locusts, and grasshoppers, which are all very common insects.

Ants are wonderful creatures. Some of them even do the same kinds of work as men do; they are builders, hunters, stock-keepers, slave-holders, and planters.

The parasol ants (or *bachacs*)* cut the leaves of certain trees and shrubs and carry them to their nests. There they prepare beds of them as gardeners do, and on these grows a fungus on which the ants live.

PARASOL ANTS.

If they are destroying your plants you should search for them at night, when you will see long lines of the little brown insects carrying pieces of

* "Wee-wees" in Belize.

leaves like parasols or umbrellas over their heads. They can then easily be followed to their nest, and this should be destroyed during the daytime, when most of them are at home.

Hunting ants* also move in great rows and catch small animals on which they feed themselves and their young. There are ants, too, which keep other insects as cows, and draw from them juices on which they feed, just as we do the milk from the cow. There are still others which keep ants of another kind as servants or slaves.

STINGLESS BEE.

Bees are a very interesting set of insects. The honey bees, which first came from Europe, live together in large numbers like a huge family, and store up honey for food. When the colony becomes too large, part of it flies away and forms a new family. In this habit ants and bees are very much alike.

* "Marching army ants" in Belize.

There are also native bees—that is, bees which have always lived in the West Indies since they were first known. Some of them are stingless.

The mosquito spends its early life in water, where it lays its eggs. In a very short time, often in one day, out of each egg comes a *larva,* a small wriggling creature like a little worm. Soon this changes into a *pupa,* with a very big head, and after that it becomes the mosquito which you all know.

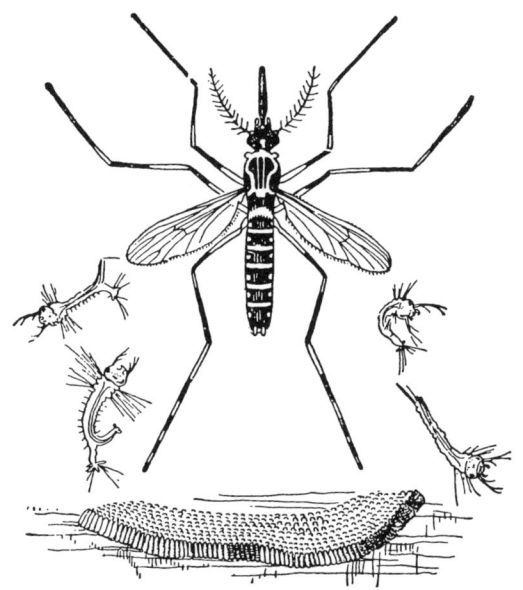

MOSQUITO, WITH LARVÆ AND PUPÆ, AND FLOATING MASS OF EGGS.

Locusts and grasshoppers have two pairs of wings, which are folded like a fan one under the other when the insect is at rest. Locusts do much damage in many parts of the world. We often hear of great hosts of them on the Main in Venezuela.

Exercises

1. Were any bees here when Columbus came? Do you think his men found honey? Why?
2. The mosquito often lays its eggs in the leaves of the "wild pine." Why do you think it does so?
3. How many wings has a locust? Catch one and make a drawing of it.
4. Why do you look for bachacs with a lantern?
5. In what ways are ants like men?
6. "Stingless" means "without sting." What other words do you know which end in "-less" meaning "without"?

LESSON 17

SPONGE-FISHING

Perhaps you often clean your slate with a sponge. Have you ever wondered where this soft yellow substance comes from, and what it really is? Of course, if you live in the Bahamas you will know quite well; but if not, this lesson will tell you.

The sponge is really a little animal which lives on the bed of the sea. It does not move about like crabs and lobsters, but remains fixed in one place, like a parasite or orchid on a tree. You can see some of them in the picture below.

If you could dive down to the bottom of the sea you would find that the living sponge does not look like your little yellow friend. It is coated with a black substance like tar.

SPONGES.

Sponges are found in the waters around the Bahamas. They grow in any depth from half a fathom to six or seven fathoms. As a rule, the deeper the water it lives in, the finer and stronger is the sponge.

Sponge-fishing provides work for many people there, and the sponge trade is the most important in the colony.

Now let us see how the fishing is done. Vessels are fitted out for sponging voyages which last from six to eight weeks. When they reach the sponging ground two men set out in a boat from the larger vessel. One of them is the oarsman and is called the "sculler," while the other fishes the sponge and is called the "hooker."

SPONGE-FISHERS AT WORK.

The picture shows them at work. The latter has a long pole and a "water-glass," which is a glass-bottomed bucket. Through this, when let down just below the ripples on the surface of the water, the bottom of the sea can be seen at almost any depth. The pole has a hook at one end with two or three prongs.

When he sees a sponge the hooker signals and the sculler stops the boat. The hooker lowers his staff until it reaches the sponge. He then fixes the hook into its roots, and with a clever twist tears it away from its lodgings.

Before taking the catch to market the crews have to clean the sponges. This takes from five to eight days.

The sponges are thrown into a "crawl" made of loose stones or stakes. There the tide washes away the black coating when it decays. The spongers beat the sponges with "gluts," or short thick clubs, and so clean out from the pores all the matter that the tides may not have washed away. If this is not done they will not sell in the market.

When the vessels return to Nassau, the sponges are sorted, counted, and sold, and then sent away to other countries to be used for many purposes.

Exercises

1. A fathom is six feet. Now fill in the numbers in these spaces. "They grow in any depth from —— to —— or —— feet."
2. The fish in the picture seems to be looking at the sponges. What colour do you think they were?
3. Sponging vessels carry several small boats on board. What are they for?
4. Fill in the blanks:

    Sponges are sold at ——.
    The —— finds the sponge.
    In each boat there is an —— who —— the ——.
    Although the —— is an animal it can be grown from cuttings.
    The laws of the Bahamas forbid fishing for sponges by drags or nets that would be likely to injure the —— where they grow.

LESSON 18

WYNKEN, BLYNKEN, AND NOD

Wynken, Blynken, and Nod one night
   Sailed off in a wooden shoe—
Sailed on a river of crystal light,
   Into a sea of dew.

"Where are you going, and what do you wish?"
  The old moon asked the three.
"We have come to fish for the herring fish
  That live in this beautiful sea;
  Nets of silver and gold have we!"
      Said Wynken,
      Blynken,
      And Nod.
The old moon laughed, and sang a song,
  As they rocked in the wooden shoe;

And the wind that sped them all night long
  Ruffled the waves of dew.
The little stars were the herring fish
  That lived in that beautiful sea.
"Now cast your nets wherever you wish;
  Never afraid are we."
So cried the stars to the fishermen three—
    Wynken,
    Blynken,
    And Nod.

All night long their nets they threw
  To the stars in the twinkling foam;
Then down from the skies came the wooden shoe,
  Bringing the fishermen home.
'Twas all so pretty a sail, it seemed
  As if it could not be,
And some folks thought 'twas a dream they'd dreamed
  Of sailing that beautiful sea;
  But I shall name you the fishermen three—
    Wynken,
    Blynken,
    And Nod.

Wynken and Blynken are two little eyes,
   And Nod is a little head,
And the wooden shoe that sailed the skies
   Is a little one's cradle-bed.
So shut your eyes while mother sings
   Of wonderful sights that be,[*]
And you shall see the beautiful things
   As you rock in the misty sea,
     Where the old shoe rocked the fishermen three—
        Wynken,
        Blynken,
        And Nod.

EUGENE FIELD.

EXERCISES

1. Who were Wynken, Blynken, and Nod?
2. Did they really sail in the sky?
3. What were the herring fish?
4. What was the wooden shoe?
5. Did Wynken, Blynken, and Nod dream?
6. Whose eyes and head were Wynken, Blynken, and Nod?
7. What were their nets made of?
8. What was the sea that they sailed in?

[*] In prose, "that *are*."

LESSON 19

THE STORY OF COLUMBUS

FIVE hundred years ago there were no Creoles, East Indians, English, French, or Spaniards in the West Indies. The people of Europe and Africa did not even know of our islands or the mainland of America.

When they looked out to the West they saw the great broad ocean stretching away as far as the eye could see. It was the vast unknown sea where no man had sailed. Men called it the "Sea of Darkness", and they spoke of it with bated breath.

They saw the sun go down behind it as behind a hill; and they thought that the wide ocean was indeed a slope down which it might be easy for a ship to glide, but which it would be impossible for her to climb again on her homeward voyage.

What a brave man he must have been who first steered his ship across the ocean, leaving all signs of land behind him! This man was Christopher Columbus.

He was the son of a weaver of Genoa, in Italy. As a sturdy, red-haired boy he loved to steal down to the sunny harbour to watch the ships come and go. When he grew up he became a clever sailor, and made voyages to England and far-off Iceland.

COLUMBUS'S SHIP, THE "SANTA MARIA".

At that time the riches of the world came from India and other countries in the East. Columbus had studied such maps as were then made, and he was one of the first to believe that the world is round, as we now know it to be. So he made up his mind to try to sail to the East by the way of the West, and go round the world to the land from which the spices came.

Being a poor man he could not get ships and men, and he tried to obtain help from several kings, but they all thought he was foolish. At last help came from the king and queen of Spain.

Three tiny ships, the *Santa Maria,* the *Pinta,* and the *Nina* were chosen for the voyage. Only the *Santa Maria* was fully decked. They were so small that we should not care to take a long journey in them today, and they could not carry much food and water. Few sailors, too, were brave enough to go out upon the "Sea of Darkness".

At last the sails of the little vessels were hoisted on the morning of the 3rd August, in the year 1492, and the tiny fleet steered away to the south-west. On and on they went for six weeks, while the sailors grumbled and wanted to put back. All they saw was the same clear blue of the sky, the white clouds driving across it, and the blue-green of the leaping waves.

Then the ships entered a sea where for long miles there is a mass of seaweed gathered together, and the crews feared the ships would stick fast. Food and water too were running short. How they wished they had never left Spain!

Not long afterwards, however, they saw some birds, and they felt sure that land could not be far away. Then the *Pinta* fished up a piece of cane and a log of wood, and the *Nina* caught a branch covered with fresh green leaves.

Late one night Columbus saw a light far across the water, and in the early morning of the 12th October the sailor on the lookout cried, "Land ahead!" There, sure enough, lay an island only a few miles away. The natives called it Guanahani. Columbus named it San Salvador, but we know it as Watling Island, one of the Bahamas.

The brave sailor had reached the islands off the coast of America, although he did not know that. He felt sure he had come to India by way of the West, and so the islands have since been known as the West Indies.

After staying some time he set sail for home, where he told the king and queen his wonderful

COLUMBUS LANDING IN THE NEW WORLD
(From the picture by Puebla.)

story of the islands on the other side of the "Sea of Darkness".

He made three more voyages, and found many more of our islands and the mainland of America. You will read more of them, and of the people he found living here, in other lessons.

Exercises

1. Take 1492 away from the date of this year. What does the answer tell you?
2. Use a calendar to find out how many days it took Columbus to reach the New World.
3. If you were sailing near the Bahamas after dark you would see a little light gleaming from a lighthouse standing on a hill on Watling Island. Do you think this was the light which Columbus saw? If not, what light do you think it was that he saw?
4. Fill in the blanks:

    Columbus was an ——.

    The *Santa Maria* was wrecked, and the other —— ships returned to Spain.

    He took the land for the king and queen and set up the flag of ——.

    Columbus saw what he thought were mermaids in the water. They were really —— or sea-cows.

    The crews said to him, "Are there no graves in —— that you bring us here to ——?"

LESSON 20

GRASSES

Grasses form the chief food of cattle and horses. Our pastures and savannahs are covered with savannah and devil grass, on which they love to graze. We also feed them on Guinea grass and Para grass, which we cut as it is wanted. Elephant grass, which comes from the Indian jungle, is now also planted for the same purpose. In Barbados sour grass is much used for pasture. It is also dried and used as hay.

In our gardens we like to have nice grassy lawns. They need much care in the wet weather to keep the grass short and green. In the dry weather it gets quite brown, but the roots do not die. After a few showers of rain it is surprising to see how quickly the lawns and pastures become green again.

Grasses differ very much in size and appearance. Our largest is the bamboo, and what a useful plant it is! Furniture, houses, bridges, fences, baskets, beads, and paper are but a few of the things we can think of as being made from it.

LESSON 20

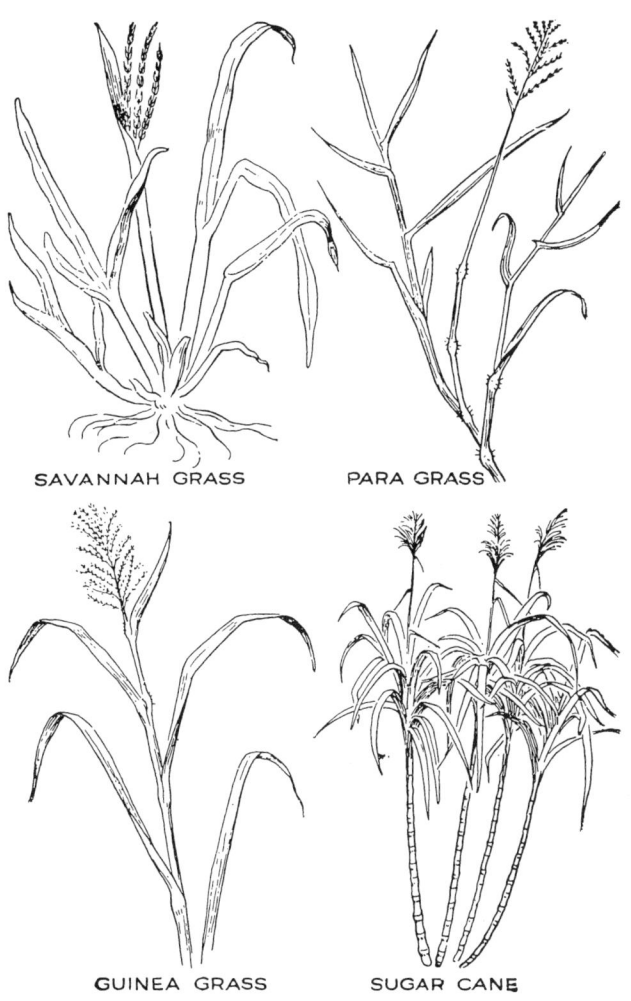

SOME WEST-INDIAN GRASSES.

We even cut the large ones into lengths for flower pots. How tall they grow and how quickly! The fibrous roots are so thickly matted together that bamboos are often planted on steep slopes to prevent the land slipping.

The sugar-cane is another kind of grass. Unlike most of the others it has a solid stem, from which the juice is squeezed out for making sugar. All of you have often enjoyed sucking a piece of sugar-cane.

We use the seeds of some kinds of grasses as food. These are called cereals, such as wheat (from which we get flour), barley, oats, rice and maize or Indian corn. The last two grow in our islands, and how pretty the bright green, swampy rice-fields look!

The corn plant is well known to us. As soon as the rainy weather comes we plant a few grains here and there, so that we may have green corn for boiling and roasting before the chief crop comes. Corn prepared in various ways forms an important article of food in many countries. We plant large fields of it, and it only takes four or five months to grow and get dry enough to reap. The grains of corn are the largest of all the cereals, and they grow around a cob. We like to see two or three cobs on each plant closely packed with grains from top to bottom.

Some grasses give much trouble to planters and farmers when growing as weeds amongst crop plants. Devil grass, Gamelot grass, Johnston grass and Para grass are the worst kinds. These are very difficult to get rid of in cacao or sugar-cane fields, and large sums of money are spent by estates every year in weeding them out.

A common wayside grass is known as tapia. It is mixed with mud to form the walls of houses, and is also used for stuffing mattresses.

Two plants which are often called grasses belong to different families. These are the nut grass, which is a sedge, and the cockroach, water grass, or pond grass, which is closely related to the oyster plant. This plant runs along the ground, forms roots at every joint, and bears a small but pretty blue flower.

Exercises

1. Write out all the names of plants mentioned in this lesson which are grasses. How many are there?
2. What grasses are useful in other ways than for our food? Name the other ways in which each one is useful.
3. Fill in these blanks:
    (a) The grasses of which we use the seeds for food are called ——.
    (b) Some grasses are pests to the planters. They are ——, ——, —— and ——.
    (c) Bamboos are often planted on steep slopes because —— —— grow —— together, and so —— the land slipping.
    (d) Sugar-cane is unlike most grasses because it has —— —— ——.

LESSON 21

A VOYAGE TO LONDON

In Lesson 19 you read of the first voyage from Europe to the West Indies. It was made by Columbus in a small caravel or sailing-ship which took ten weeks to cross the ocean. Ships have changed much since then, and one of the big liners, such as the Harrison, Elders and

Fyffes, French or Dutch, now makes the journey in about two weeks.

Let us suppose we are going to London, the capital of the United Kingdom, in one of these steamers, and that we have sailed to Barbados to join it there. Perhaps you would keep a diary or short account of what you do every day. If so, it might read something like this:

First Day.—We have now been steaming away from the West Indies for several hours, and all sign of land has disappeared. There is a steady breeze blowing against us, but the powerful engines of our ship send it onwards all the time. Some of the passengers are feeling sea-sick as the big liner rolls about in the waves.

Second Day.—How lovely the sea looks this morning! It seems to have taken on a deeper blue tint, which stands out against the clear light blue of the sky. The sun shines brightly and every one on board is happy. Some people are playing games on the deck of the ship. What are those creatures flitting about on the

AN OCEAN LINER.
Insets.—Funnels of chief lines which call at the West Indies: 1. Harrison; 2. Elders And Fyffes; 3. French; 4. Dutch; 5. Hamburg-Amerika; 6. Canadian National Steamships.

surface of the water like dragon-flies? Oh! they are flying-fish. How pretty their glistening wings appear as they dart out of the water!

Third Day.—The breeze is still blowing against us. There was great excitement this morning when the look-out spied a stream of water rising high into the air. It was a whale which had come up to "blow" or breathe. We could see his big dark body in the water. This is the only thing we saw all day except the sea and sky around us.

Fourth Day.—Early this morning I saw some bright yellow weed in the sea. As the day wore on, the patches of it grew bigger, until there seemed to be masses of it on the surface of the water. This is the Gulf Weed that the crew of Columbus saw. It is always to be found in this part of the ocean.

Fifth Day.—Today the sea is quite calm as the breeze seems to have died away. About midday we saw a ship far away on the starboard side. She drew near and crossed our bows not far ahead, when we could make out she was an oil-tanker.

It feels nice to know we are not the only ship on this vast expanse of water.

Sixth Day.—The air is now chilly, and we, who are used to living in the sunny lands of the West Indies, begin to feel cold. We must put on some thicker underclothing. There are no flying-fish or Gulf Weed to be seen now.

AN OIL-TANKER.

Seventh Day.—The breeze has risen again, but it has turned round, and is now blowing gently behind us. Today I went all over the ship, up to the captain's bridge, on the boat-deck, into the saloons and cabins, and down to the engine-room. What a wonderful ship it is, and how much more pleasant it must be crossing the ocean in this palace than it was for Columbus and his men in their small vessels.

Eighth Day.—At nine o'clock this morning I could see a grey mass ahead, and by noon we were abreast of it. It was the first land we had seen for over seven days, and was an island—one of the Azores. Our ship does not call there, or we might see pineapples being grown in glass houses. The ladies wear a strange hood or capote.

PINEAPPLES GROWING IN A GLASS HOUSE.

Ninth Day.—This has been a very dull, wet day, and as it is growing still colder I kept inside the cosy saloon.

Tenth Day.—The wind is now quite strong behind us, and the captain says we have sailed 280 sea miles today. We shall soon be at the end of our long journey.

THE WHITE CLIFFS OF DOVER.

Eleventh Day.—The sea is now very rough. We are near the Bay of Biscay, and as I am not a good sailor, I stayed in my cabin.

Twelfth Day.—Land ahead! There is the coastline of England with its white cliffs standing up out of the sea.

Thirteenth Day.—We have sailed steadily up the English Channel and have seen several big liners starting off to all parts of the world.

Fourteenth Day.—Here we are at last in the Thames. Our liner is taken into the docks by two tugs, and how glad we are to step on land again after two weeks in our home on the sea! But how cold it seems to us! We must hasten to buy thicker coats before setting out to see something of this great city of London.

Exercises

1. What is a diary? Write a diary showing what you have done this week.
2. How long does it take to go to England?
3. Where are the following seen on the journey: flying-fish, Gulf Weed, land, and many ships?
4. What liners come to the West Indies from England? How do you know to what line they belong? Draw the funnels of each line, and colour them.

IN A LONDON DOCK.

LESSON 22

WINDS

Like the sea, the air is nearly always in motion. Air in motion is wind. If the motion is slight, it is a breeze; if very violent, it is a storm, tempest, or hurricane.

We cannot see the air moving, but we can feel it, and we can see the effects of its motion. We see the trees bend, and hear their leaves rustle in the wind; we see the clouds moving slowly across the sky in a gentle breeze, or flying before the storm; and we see the waves raised by the wind on the surface of water.

Winds in the air are like rivers on land. Just as water flows in the bed of a river, so great currents of air, or winds, flow over the land and the sea.

One great difference between rivers and currents of air is that rivers continue for a very long time to flow in the same direction, while winds constantly change their direction.

Air currents are much larger, too, than any river. They may be hundreds of miles wide and of very great depth. We must not think, however, that the wind which we feel is also blowing high up in the air, or that it is calm high up because it is so on the surface of the earth.

Sometimes there are, at the same time, two currents of air, one above the other, moving in different directions—one, perhaps, from north to south, the other from south to north. When we feel no wind we can often see the clouds moving rapidly high up in the sky.

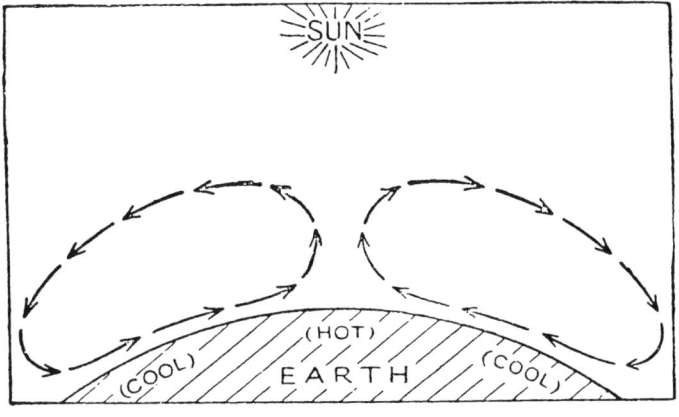

UPPER AND LOWER CURRENTS OF AIR.

Before the invention of the steam-engine men made more use of the wind than they do now.

Ships moved by its help, and mills for grinding cane were turned by it. Now nearly all the large ships are steamers, and cane-mills are often driven by steam-engines.

Why does not the air always remain calm? Why are there any winds? Winds are largely caused by the heat of the sun. Let us try to understand how this can be.

We have already learned that as water evaporates, the water-vapour so formed rises into the air. We know that this is so when water is heated, because we see the steam which comes from it rising into the air. Why does it rise?

Simply because it is lighter than the air. If we hold a piece of wood under water and then let it go, it will rise to the top of the water. It does so because it is lighter than the water. In the same way the water-vapour rises because it is lighter than the air.

Now, just as heat changes water into water-vapour, which is lighter than air, so heat makes the air itself lighter; and so warm air will always rise above air which is colder, and cold air will sink, or fall, through that which is warmer.

Now the air over the land is heated by the sun much more rapidly than the air over the sea. Hot air, therefore, rises from the land. This rising of the warm air makes room for other air to take its place, and a current of air or a wind flows from the sea towards the land.

People who live on the coast notice that a sea breeze often begins to blow about noon, and becomes stronger till after sunset, when it dies away; a land breeze rises in the cool early morning, and dies away towards noon.

SEA BREEZE.

You now understand the cause of the sea breeze. The land breeze is caused in a similar way. During the night the air over the land becomes cool more rapidly than the air over the sea, and therefore air from the land is made to flow over the sea; this is the land breeze.

We see, then, that winds are often caused by the heat of the sun, and that they often flow from the sea to the land. The winds that come from the sea are laden with moisture, which is carried over the land by the wind, and falls as much-needed rain.

When you grow older you will learn why our winds nearly always blow from the east, and why most of our rain falls in one part of the year—the wet season.

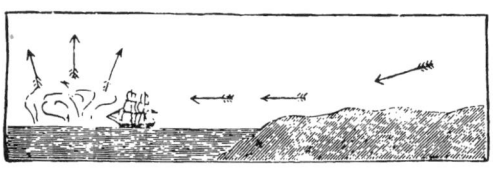

LAND BREEZE.

Exercises

1. What is wind?
2. How do we know that wind may be blowing high up when it is calm on the earth?
3. What is now used to propel ships?
4. What are winds largely caused by?
5. What makes air lighter?
6. When does the sea breeze blow?
7. Write the opposite of these words: Rise, windy, evaporate, sea breeze, heat, lighter, sunset, noon.

LESSON 23

THE MONKEY AND THE ALLIGATOR

A CREOLE FOLK-TALE

One day a monkey was climbing about in a balata tree looking for fruit. An alligator, who was lying on a mud flat at the root of the tree, with his mouth open, catching flies, asked the monkey in a friendly way what he was doing.

"Looking for balata to eat," said the monkey, "but they are very scarce up here."

"Well, now, I saw a tree full of them as I was coming up the river this morning," said the alligator.

"Really," replied the hungry one, "but how can I get to them?"

"Oh, that is very easy," answered his artful friend. "If you are not afraid to get on my back, I can soon swim there with you."

"But," said Mr. Monkey, becoming suspicious, "suppose you dive and let me down into the river, I'd hate to get my feet wet."

"Oh, no fear of that, my friend," returned Mr. Alligator.

The monkey, being very hungry, took the risk; he climbed down and perched carefully on the reptile's back. All went well for a time, the little animal keeping a sharp look-out for the fruit-laden tree, but as none appeared he asked: "Where did you see that tree, my friend?"

"Well, to tell you the truth, sir," the artful alligator replied, "I didn't see a tree."

Hearing this the monkey felt uneasy, and inquired, "Then where are you taking me to?"

"Well, my son, my wife is very ill and the doctor says she must have monkey liver soup, so I am taking you home to her," answered Mr. Alligator.

Now, the monkey, seeing the danger he was in, became artful too, and said, "I am very sorry, friend, that your wife is sick, and I would gladly help her, but I haven't my liver with me."

"How is that?" asked the alligator.

"Well, you see, there was something the matter with it, so I took it out this morning to wash it, and it is now hanging up to dry in the tree I came from," said he.

"Upon my word," replied the reptile, "how could you be so careless as to leave it there?"

"But," added the monkey, "I should not like your wife to be disappointed, so if you will swim back to the tree, I can easily go up and get it for you."

"Do you mean that?" asked the alligator.

"Of course I do," answered the monkey.

So they quickly returned to the place from which they started, and the monkey, with a joyful heart, landed and skipped up the tree. He was long in coming down, so his friend shouted up to him, "Have you got it?"

"Oh yes," said Mr. Monkey. "I had it all the time, but I prefer to keep it for myself."

The alligator was so overcome at being tricked by the monkey that he wept, and ever since, when he thinks of it, the tears come to his eyes.

Exercises

1. Which was the mammal, and which was the reptile in this story?
2. Write out all the words in the lesson which mean "spoke".
3. How many questions are asked in the story?
4. There is an old saying which states, "He laughs best who laughs last." Which one laughed last in the story?
5. Which do you think was the more artful of the two? Why?
6. Fill in the missing words:

    "An alligator eats ——, but a monkey eats ——."

LESSON 24

ROBINSON CRUSOE

A LONG time ago a boy named Robinson Crusoe lived with his parents at Hull, a great seaport on the east coast of England. He wished very much to be a sailor, so one day he ran away to sea.

On one of his voyages a great storm arose, and the ship ran on the rocks near an island far away in the ocean. People say this island was Tobago, one of the West Indies. It is often called Crusoe's Island. All the crew were drowned except Crusoe, and he was cast up by the waves on the rocky shore, more dead than alive.

When morning came, he saw that the sea was now quite calm, and that the wreck lay about a mile from the shore. He swam out to the ship, and got on board by means of a rope that was hanging over the side. Then he set to work and made a raft out of a number of spars. On this raft he placed food, tools, guns, powder, shot, and other things which he found in the ship. Then he pushed off for the shore. Time after time he went to the ship on his raft, and he brought ashore most of the useful things in the wreck.

At first he set up a tent near the shore and lived for some time in it, but he soon made a better home for himself in a cave. He fenced it in with stakes, and inside the fence he put all the things which he had taken from the wreck. There was no door in the fence, and Crusoe went in and out of his home by means of a ladder.

After he had been some time on the island, he set up a large post and carved on it these words: "I came on shore here on the 20th of September 1659." Upon the side of this post he cut a notch every day, so that he might know when it was Sunday. He found plenty of work to do. He spent his long, lonely days and evenings in making chairs and tables for his house, and many other things for his comfort and safety.

One day he was roaming about with a dog which had been saved from the wreck, when he found a young kid that had lost its mother. The dog would have killed the kid, but Crusoe caught

"Going towards the boat I was exceedingly surprised with the print of a man's naked foot on the shore."

it and brought it home. In time it became a great pet and followed him about wherever he went.

He had now for company his dog, four cats, and a parrot, all saved from the wreck, as well as the young goat. After a while he began to teach the parrot to talk. He quickly taught it to say its own name, "Poll". It was a great comfort to talk to the parrot and to have the parrot talk to him.

A little later he made a boat in the woods, out of the trunk of a tree which he felled. It was a fine boat, but it was so heavy that he could not get it down to the sea. From this he learned a lesson, and his next boat was made at the water's edge. He fitted it with a mast and a sail, and fixed up an umbrella in the stern to shade him from the heat of the sun. In this boat he sailed right round his island home.

Crusoe had brought some shirts and coats from the wreck; but the coats soon wore out, and he set to work to make new clothes. He saved the skins of the animals that he shot, and out of these skins he made what he wanted. He also made a great skin umbrella to shade him from the rays of the sun.

Crusoe lived fifteen years on the island without seeing a human being. Then one day he saw the print of a man's naked foot on the sand. This made him afraid, and he went home as quickly as he could. That night he slept little, for he now knew that there were savages on the island, and he feared that they might kill him at any moment.

His first care was to make his house secure. He set up a wooden wall outside his fence. In this wall he cut seven holes, and in each hole he fixed one of the guns he had brought from the wreck. The guns were so placed that he could fire all seven of them in a short time.

Before long, he found that a certain tribe of savages used to visit the island. Early one morning he saw five canoes on the shore, and through his spy-glass he saw the savages making ready for a feast. They had with them a number of prisoners taken in war, and these they began to kill and eat. Crusoe saved the life of one of their

ROBINSON CRUSOE IN HIS CAVE.
(*Alexander Fraser, A.R.S.A.*)

prisoners, who made his escape from them. He called him Friday, because that was the day of the week on which he first saw him. Friday was very quick and very willing to learn, and became a great help to his master.

While Crusoe and Friday were working one day, they saw that another savage feast was going to take place. There were three poor fellows lying bound on the beach, and one of them was a white man. At once Crusoe set out to save them from their cruel fate. The white man turned out to be a Spaniard. Meanwhile, Friday, to his great joy, found that one of the prisoners was his own father!

At last one day a boat came ashore with eleven white men in it. Three of them were bound with ropes. The crew of a passing ship had risen against their officers, and were putting them ashore on what they thought was a desert island. Crusoe helped the officers to overcome the crew and get command of their ship once more. Having done this, he went on board the ship and left the island on which he had lived so long. He went back to England, and all who heard his story were filled with wonder at the strange life he had led so long.

You can read the full story in the book called *Robinson Crusoe*.

Exercises

1. Study the picture on page ii and then that on page 107. What difference do you notice in the dress of Robinson Crusoe in the two pictures?
2. How did he make the clothes which he is wearing on page 107? Of what is he thinking?
3. Robinson Crusoe was born in the year 1632. He landed on the island in the year 1659. He left the island in the year 1687. How old was he when he landed on the island? How many years was he on the island? How old was he when he left the island?
4. How did Robinson Crusoe know how long he had been on the island?

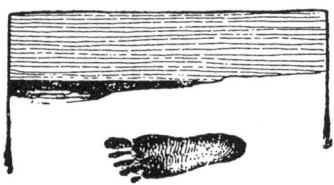

LESSON 25

EXERCISE

THE third health lesson I have to learn is this—*I must take plenty of exercise*. To make the body strong we must use it. The parts that are most used become the strongest, and those we use least will be the weakest.

The arms of the blacksmith are very strong because he uses them so much. Ours are weaker than his because we use them so much less. The man who works at healthful labour becomes strong, while the idle man becomes weak.

The boy who works and plays in the open air grows strong and healthy, but the boy who sits indoors and does not take exercise grows up to be a weak and unhealthy man. It is best to take our exercise in the open air and the sunlight.

Games like football and cricket are good for boys. There are also plenty of pleasant outdoor games for girls. When no game can be played, a brisk walk in the open air is quite as good. Brisk walking is one of the easiest and best of exercises, both for boys and for girls.

But there are some things we should avoid when taking exercise. We should not work or play too long without resting. We should not try to do things that are beyond our strength. When exercise is too violent, it does harm rather than good.

A king, who was feeble and ill because of idleness, asked his doctor for medicine. The doctor was wiser than the king, and knew that it was not medicine but healthful exercise that he needed.

He might have told him that it was his own laziness which had injured his health. But he knew very well that the king would not believe this, and he was very much afraid of making him angry.

The doctor therefore brought the king two heavy clubs of a strange kind of wood, and told him that these clubs held the medicine for his cure.

The doctor told him that he must grasp them by the handles and swing them about till his hands became moist from the exercise, and this moisture would make the medicine act. He obeyed the faithful doctor, and each day he might be seen in the open air at certain hours, working manfully with his magic clubs.

His muscles grew strong, his health improved, and he greatly praised the medicine of his clubs and the wisdom of his good doctor. The king never learned that the clubs were nothing but wood, and that the secret of their wonderful cure was found not in the clubs but in his own healthful exercise with them.

Clubs of this sort are often used by boys and young men, and by girls also, to make their hands and arms strong. We call them Indian clubs. Dumb-bells, made of wood or of iron, are also used for the same purpose. In many of our schools the children get drill with dumb-bells or Indian clubs, to help in making their bodies healthy and strong.

Exercises

1. What was inside the king's clubs?
2. What should we *not* do when taking exercise?
3. Why are games good for boys and girls?
4. What had made the king ill?
5. Why do children drill in schools?
6. How many men are mentioned in this lesson? Who were they?

LESSON 26

THE MOCK TURTLE'S SONG

"Will you walk a little faster?" said a whiting* to a snail.
"There's a porpoise close behind us, and he's treading on my tail.
See how eagerly the lobsters and the turtles all advance!
They are waiting on the shingle†—will you come and join the dance?
Will you, won't you, will you, won't you, won't you join the dance?

"You can really have no notion how delightful it will be,

---

* A *whiting* is a small fish about the size of a grunt.
† The *shingle* is the small stones on the seashore.

When they take us up and throw us, with
  the lobsters, out to sea!"
But the snail replied, "Too far, too far!"
  and gave a look askance—
Said he thanked the whiting kindly, but he would
  not join the dance.
Would not, could not, would not, could not,
  could not join the dance.

"What matters it how far we go?" his
  scaly friend replied;
"There is another shore, you know, upon
  the other side.
The farther off from England the nearer is
  to France—
Then turn not pale, belovèd snail, but come and
  join the dance.
Will you, won't you, will you, won't you, won't
  you join the dance?"

Lewis Carroll.
(*From "Alice in Wonderland"*)

Exercises

1. How many things that live in the sea are mentioned in this poem?
2. How many that live on the land?
3. How many are supposed to be speaking? Who were they?
4. Who is the "scaly friend"? Why?
5. Why did not the snail want to join the dance?
6. How many questions are asked in these verses?

LESSON 27

FRUIT TREES

If we wish to keep in good health we must eat plenty of fresh fruit and vegetables.

In the West Indies we can get fruit all the year round. In cold countries it does not ripen during the winter, and the people who live there are glad to get oranges, bananas, and pineapples from warmer countries.

There are many kinds of fruit trees in the West Indies. Some are native, and others have been brought from different parts of the world. Most of our fruit trees are evergreen—that is, they are never without leaves. In cold countries the trees are generally bare of leaves in the winter. They are not of the same kinds as ours.

Our commonest fruit is the mango. It came from India, but now grows wild. There are many kinds. You will know some of them by the names mango vert, mango rose, zabricot, and calabash. These, however, are not the best kinds. They are known by such names as Julie, Peters, and Gordon, and are called grafted mangoes. This is because the plants are grafted instead of being raised from seed. You will learn how this is done when you are older.

MANGO.

BANANAS.

Bananas or figs are largely grown. Sometimes the plants are used as shade for young cacao or coffee trees. In Jamaica large quantities of bananas are grown to send to England and America. They are packed in the holds of ships, which are kept specially cool for this purpose. One ship will carry as many as 70,000 bunches.

SUGAR-APPLE.

Oranges, grapefruit, and limes are known by the general name of citrus fruits. Most of those called sweet oranges grow amongst other crops such as cacao. There are other kinds which are more suitable for packing and shipping. Two of these are known by the names Navel and Jaffa. These are grown by people who wish to send fruit abroad. For this purpose the trees must be very carefully tended.

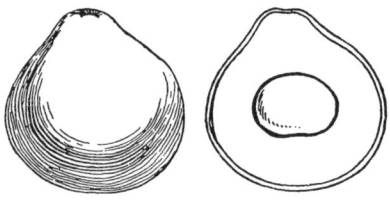

AVOCADO—FRUIT AND SECTION.

Limes are the chief crop in Dominica, and in all the islands most people have at least one lime tree in their garden.

In the drier parts of the West Indies we find sugar-apples and custard-apples. They have very

PAPAW.

sweet pulp, as have also sapodillas and star-apples, which grow in moist places.

GUAVA.

The zaboca, avocado, or alligator pear has a nutty and buttery flavour. Unlike most other fruits it is best eaten with salt, pepper, and vinegar. Because of this it is called a salad fruit, as are also cucumbers and tomatoes.

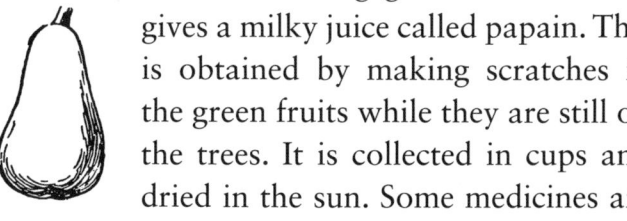

BREADFRUIT.   CASHEW.

The fruit of the papaw looks somewhat like a water-melon. Besides being good to eat it also

gives a milky juice called papain. This is obtained by making scratches in the green fruits while they are still on the trees. It is collected in cups and dried in the sun. Some medicines are
POMMERAC. made from it.

Guavas are very plentiful in most of the West Indian Islands. From them the well-known guava jelly and guava cheese are made.

The breadfruit, which is now a common article of food, is not native. It has a very interesting history. In the year 1787, Captain Bligh sailed to the South Sea Islands, in a ship named the *Bounty*, for the purpose of getting breadfruit plants. When he was on his way to the West Indies with them, the crew mutinied and the plants were lost. Bligh and some of his men were set adrift in an open boat, but after a wonderful voyage of more than three thousand miles they reached safety.

In 1793 another attempt was made by Captain Bligh in a ship called the *Providence*. This time he was successful, and landed his plants in St. Vincent. These were grown in the Botanic Gardens, and plants were afterwards sent to the other islands. The people did not care much for the breadfruit at first, and preferred the plantain.

There are many other kinds of fruits which you know well. There are the cashew, the akee, the genip, the golden apple, the pommerac or pomme malac, the soursop and several kinds of West Indian plums.

Exercises

Fill in the blanks:
1. The best kinds of mangoes are not raised from seeds but are ———.
2. The ships which take bananas to England have to be ——— ———.
3. Limes, ——— and ——— are called citrus fruit.
4. ——— and ——— grow where it is dry, but ——— and ——— like damp places.
5. From the juice of the papaw a kind of ——— is made. It is called ———.
6. The breadfruit was first grown in the West Indies in the island of ———. It came from the——— ———.
7. Eating fruit and vegetables keeps us ———.

AKEE.

LESSON 28

A COUNTRY OF FORESTS

You have read that Trinidad, Guyana, Barbados, and Jamaica are noted for their sugar, Trinidad and Grenada for cocoa, Jamaica for bananas, coffee, and tobacco, St. Vincent for arrowroot, Dominica for limes, Montserrat for cotton, Grenada for spices such as nutmegs and mace, the Cayman Islands for turtles, the Bahamas for sponges, and Guyana for gold, diamonds, rice, and balata rubber.

There is another Commonwealth country on the Main where the chief thing produced is the wood from the forests. This is Belize. It is bigger than Barbados, Jamaica, Trinidad, the Windward and the Leeward Islands put together.

Perhaps you have been in some of the forests of your own island, and they have seemed very vast, with huge monsters of trees growing in them. They would look very small if they were placed by the side of the forests of Belize, which cover the greater part of that big country.

For over two hundred years the giants of the forest, mahogany trees, have been cut down and sent away to other countries to be made into furniture. Of course this was first done near the rivers, where the logs could be floated down to the coast to be shipped. Now the logs have to be taken to the streams for long distances by oxen or by motor-tractors, which are known as caterpillars. You can see one of them in the picture.

CATERPILLAR MOTOR-TRACTOR.

In the rainy season, when the rivers are full, the big heavy logs will float down easily. The picture on page 127 shows you some of them chained together as rafts on their way down the Belize river. Such a sight as this can never be seen in any of the islands, where the forests and rivers are much smaller than in Belize.

Although mahogany is the chief wood, others, such as rosewood, cedar, logwood, fustic and sapodilla, are found in the forests. The sap or milk which is drawn from the sapodilla tree is known as chicle, and is made into chewing-gum. Pine trees are found in some parts, and they are cut up in the local saw-mills.

You may like to know that much mahogany from these forests was used during the Great War in the building of aeroplanes.

Wild animals, such as the jaguar and puma, roam through these forests, and reptiles, such as snakes and lizards of many kinds, are often seen. Iguanas live in the trees along the river-banks. In March they lay their eggs in holes which they make in sandy places along the banks. The natives search for the eggs, and eat them as well as the reptiles themselves.

If you tried to journey through the forest off the paths or tracks which are made by the woodcutters, you would find it very difficult.

RAFT OF LOGS, BELIZE RIVER.

Lianas, or "tie-ties," spread themselves like a great network from tree to tree. A sharp cutlass or machete would be needed to make a pathway.

Exercises

1. Write out the names of all the countries given in this lesson. Learn to spell them properly.
2. Why do you think the tractors are called "caterpillars"?
3. Why do you think the lianas are called "tie-ties"?
4. What are the *giants* of the forest? What could you call the *dwarfs* in a forest?
5. Write out all the words in the lesson which mean *big* or *big things*.

LESSON 29

A BRIDGE OF CROCODILES

ON a lovely island in the middle of the Amazon, that great river on the Main, there once lived a lonely monkey. There was little for him to do on this island, and he had no friends there. So he often sat on the shore, and longed and sighed for some means of getting across the water to his friends on the mainland, for the river was many miles wide at that point.

One day he saw a big crocodile swimming near the shore of the island. "Ah," thought the monkey, "I will ask this big fellow to carry me across the river and put me on the mainland." Then, being full of mischief, he made up his mind that he would play a trick upon the crocodile.

"Oh, my dear Mr. Crocodile," he cried out, "isn't this lovely weather? Won't you come on land and have a game with me?"

So the crocodile, who felt a trifle lonely on that bright sunny day, came out of the water and played games with the monkey.

They romped together for some time, and they were very happy as they jumped and ran, and played at leapfrog and hopscotch.

After a time they grew tired, and sat down to rest. Then the monkey, who meant to play his trick upon the crocodile, said—

"Tell me, my dear Mr. Crocodile, are there more crocodiles in the world than monkeys?"

"Ho, ho, ho!" laughed the crocodile, who was very conceited. "My dear Mr. Monkey, what a stupid question! Of course there are more crocodiles in the world than monkeys—ever so many more."

"Well, then," said the cunning monkey, "are there enough crocodiles to make a bridge from this island to the mainland? I don't think so."

"Really, really!" cried the crocodile, "What nonsense you do talk! There are more than enough crocodiles to reach from here to the mainland and back again."

"I don't believe it," said the monkey.

"Then I will just show you," answered the crocodile.

With that he gave a great shout, and soon, far out in the stream, there was a boiling and a bubbling. It seemed as if a great storm was coming towards the island, and the water was white with foam.

As the splashing came nearer the monkey could see the ugly black snouts of hundreds of crocodiles sticking out of the water. When they came close to the shore they stopped, as if they were waiting for orders.

"There, Mr. Monkey," said the crocodile, "did you ever see so many splendid fellows in your life?"

"It is a grand sight," replied the monkey. "But do you really think that there are enough to reach from here to the mainland? I doubt it."

"We will soon see about that," said the crocodile, and he roared out another order. Then all the crocodiles began swimming out in the river, placing themselves in line, snout to tail, as they went, until the end of the line was lost in the blue distance.

"Capital! capital!" cried the monkey, clapping his forepaws. "But I should like to be quite sure that the farthest crocodile is really touching the mainland. Steady, Mr. Crocodiles!" he cried. "I am going to run across your backs. I want to count you."

So saying, the monkey hopped on to the back of the first crocodile, and walked across that strange bridge until he reached the mainland. When he was safely on shore he laughed, and danced, and jeered.

"Ha, ha! you stupid old crocodiles," he shouted, "go away home to your dinners. I didn't want to count you at all; I wanted to get to the mainland. And, now I am here, I have no more use for you."

Then the crocodiles set up a great roar, and began swimming towards the shore, lashing the water with their tails. The monkey tried to run away, but the crocodiles were too quick for him. They seized him, and began to pull out his fur.

"Oh, I am so sorry," squealed the monkey. "Please let me go!"

But with each tuft of fur they pulled out the crocodiles said, "It serves you right, you sly monkey." Then they went back into the water, leaving the poor naked monkey lying on the beach.

What do you think happened next? If your teacher obtains a little book called *Tales from Japan* you will be able to hear the rest. The Japanese story is told of a hare instead of a monkey.

Adapted from CAPTAIN BLUECOAT'S
"Tales from Japan"

EXERCISES

1. Compare this story with that given in Lesson 23.
    (*a*) Which do you prefer? Why?
    (*b*) In what ways are the two stories alike?

(c) How do they differ?
(d) Who laughed last in this story?
(e) In what way were the monkeys alike in the two stories?
2. Fill in the missing words:
   (a) The island was in the continent of ———.
   (b) The monkey was ———, but the crocodile was ———.
   (c) The reptiles' noses were ——— and ———.
   (d) The bridge was a very ——— one, but it ——— him to get to the mainland.
3. Write out all the words in the lesson which mean "spoke".

LESSON 30

LULLABY OF AN INFANT CHIEF

Introduction.—This is a lullaby, or song sung by a mother to her child to make him sleep. The child's father is dead, and therefore the castle in which he lives, and the land round it, are his own. In time he will be a man, and will have to fight; but now he can sleep safely, because there are many soldiers in the castle to guard him.

O HUSH thee, my baby, thy sire was a knight,
Thy mother a lady, both lovely and bright;

The woods and the glens from the towers which we see,
They all are belonging, dear baby, to thee.

O fear not the bugle, though loudly it blows;
It calls but the warders that guard thy repose;
Their bows would be bended,* their blades would be red,
Ere the step of a foeman draws near to thy bed.

O hush thee, my baby, the time soon will come
When thy sleep shall be broken by trumpet and drum;

---

* In prose, *bent*.

Then hush thee, my darling, take rest while you may,
For strife comes with manhood, and waking with day.

Sir Walter Scott.

Exercises

1. Why do the woods and glens belong to the baby?
2. Where are the mother and the baby?
3. What does the bugle blow for?
4. Why would the warders' blades be red?
5. What will in time break the baby's sleep?
6. Why will it be so broken?
7. What comes with manhood?
8. Does it come to people who are not soldiers?

LESSON 31

PANDORA'S BOX

Once upon a time there were two playmates—a little girl named Pandora and a little boy named Epimetheus. In those days there were no old people in the world; it was a world of children. There was no hard work to be done and no lessons to be learned, so you may know that life was very pleasant.

When the boys and the girls wanted dinner, they found it growing upon a tree. After they had eaten their food, there was nothing but sports and dances and games all the day, and sound sleep by night. No child ever sulked or got into a temper, and through all the wide, wide world there were none of those things we call troubles or cares or sorrows. So you will see that must have been a long time ago.

Now in the pretty cottage where Epimetheus lived there was a very large box, and one day Pandora said, "Epimetheus, what is in that box?"

"That is a secret, dear," said the boy gently. "I do not know myself, and the one who left it here told me that I must never ask about it."

"How silly!" said Pandora. "I wish the box could be taken away."

"Never mind," said Epimetheus, "let us go out to play."

The girl would not cease talking about the box. "Why not open it?" she said at last.

"Open it? No, no," cried Epimetheus. "We must not do that without permission." Then, because he was tired of hearing so much about the box, he went out to play with the other children, and Pandora was left alone.

After Epimetheus had left her, Pandora stood gazing at the box for a long time. It was made of dark wood, with so fine a polish that Pandora could see her face in it as in a mirror. On the middle of the lid was a curious carved creature with a beautiful woman's face. Round the box was a cord of gold which was tied in a curious knot. "It must have been a very clever person who tied that knot," said Pandora to herself. "I wonder if I could untie it."

So she took the golden string in her fingers and gave the cord a kind of twist. Then, as if by magic, the knot untied itself and left the box ready to open. Pandora now began to feel much afraid of what Epimetheus would say when he found out what she had done. So she tried to fasten the cord again, but found that she could not do so.

"What shall I do?" she cried. "If Epimetheus finds the cord untied, he will think I have looked into the box.—Then why should I not look?" she said to herself after a while.

As she sat there, she thought she heard small voices within the box saying, "Let us out, dear Pandora; pray let us out! We shall be such nice playmates for you. Please do let us out!"

"There must be something alive in the box," said the girl. "I will take one peep—just one peep—and then the lid shall be shut down as safely as ever."

Now, just as Pandora said these words Epimetheus came up to the cottage door. He had made a wreath of flowers for his playmate, and meant to steal softly behind her and slip it over her head.

When he opened the door, he saw Pandora kneeling down before the box with her back towards him. Now Epimetheus himself wished very much to know what was in the box. So instead of running forward to stop Pandora from opening it, he stood waiting to see what would happen.

As Pandora raised the lid, the cottage grew very dark, and there was a loud peal of thunder.

The girl paid no heed to these things, but lifted the lid a little higher and looked inside. Then it seemed as if a swarm of winged creatures brushed past her out of the box, and in a moment she heard Epimetheus cry, "Oh, I am stung!"

This was the first cry of pain that had ever been heard in the world!

The girl let fall the lid and stood up. In the dim light she saw a crowd of ugly little shapes with long stings in their tails flying about the room. One of them settled on her brow and would have stung her, if Epimetheus had not come up and brushed it away.

Now these ugly little things were the first Troubles which had been seen in the world. There was one called Temper, and another Sulks, and another Greed, as well as many others with names quite as ugly as themselves.

After a few moments Pandora opened the window, and the Troubles flew out into the open air. After that the children of the world were happy only now and again instead of all the time; and, instead of keeping always young, they grew up to become men and women, and at last grew old and died.

Meanwhile, Pandora had flung herself down on the floor beside the box and was sobbing as if her heart would break. All at once she heard a gentle tap on the inside of the lid. "What can that be? "she cried, raising her head.

Again the tap was heard. It sounded like a fairy's hand knocking lightly on the inside of the box.

"Who are you?" asked Pandora.

A sweet little voice called from within, "Only lift the lid and you shall see."

"No, no," said Pandora, "I will never lift that lid again. You must stay where you are."

"Ah," said the sweet little voice again, "you will be much pleased when you see me. Those naughty Troubles need some one to look after them, and I alone can do it."

"My dear Epimetheus," said Pandora turning to the boy, "what shall I do?"

"You may as well open it," said her playmate, not very kindly, "and as the lid seems heavy I will help you." So they raised the lid, and out flew a shining little person with golden hair and fairy wings. She flew to Epimetheus and touched the spot where the Trouble had stung him, and at once the pain of it was gone.

Then the bright little fairy danced round and round the children in such a merry way that they began to forget all about the Troubles with stings in their tails. "Who are you, my pretty dear?" asked Pandora at last.

"I am called Hope," said the bright fairy, "and because I am so cheery I was packed in that box with the Troubles. My work will be to follow them about and cure people whom they may hurt."

"And you will stay with us," asked Epimetheus, "for ever and ever?"

"Yes, for ever and ever," said the bright fairy, "You shall never lose sight of your little friend Hope."

*   *   *   *   *   *

This fine story is taken from a book called *Tanglewood Tales*. I am sure you will like the other stories in that book also.

"I AM CALLED HOPE."

(*Page 141.*)

Exercises

1. How do you know that this story tells of a long time ago?
2. Why did Pandora open the box?
3. What did she find inside?
4. Was Epimetheus glad she had opened it?
5. Why did Pandora open it a second time?
6. Who came out then?
7. If you could paint another picture to go with this story, what would you put in it? What colours would you use?

LESSON 32

BIRDS

The birds of some countries are famous for their song. You may have heard of the lark, the nightingale, and the thrush. Now although our birds have many calls, we can hardly say they are fine songsters. They are beautiful in another way, however, and that is in their brilliant plumage.

Many of the hundreds of kinds which live here are noted for the lovely colours of their feathers. The king of the woods, the jacamar, and even the macaw are all very beautiful creatures.

Large numbers of birds are only found here during certain seasons. They migrate or go to other countries, some to cool climates and others even to the frozen lands near the poles.

In some colonies there are laws which forbid certain birds to be killed during their nesting season, while others may not be killed at all. Your teacher will tell you if there is such a law in your colony, and which birds are protected by it.

"KING OF THE WOODS."

WHITE EGRET.

There are many water-birds in the swamps and on the sea-shore. The flamingo (*flaman*) is a long-legged and long-billed red bird. The spatule has a spoon-shaped bill. Many herons live in the swamps. One of them is the white egret (*aigrette*), which is often killed for the sake of its white plumes. It is a crime to do this.

The great bird with long wings which is often seen sailing high in the air is the frigate (*frégate*) or man-o'-war bird. It sometimes measures seven feet across the wings. Another large bird is the Muscovy duck (*canard pays*).

A rare but beautiful bird is the king corbeau. Its head and neck are orange, purple, and crimson. The upper part of its body is cream, the wings largely fawn, and the tail black. Underneath it is white and cream. As with many other birds, the female is not so brightly coloured as the male.

KING CORBEAU

Of course you know the black corbeau or vulture, sometimes called the "Johnny Crow," as it is common in towns and villages. We can hardly call him beautiful. There is yet another kind with a red head.

Hawks and owls are often seen. The latter eat many rats, mice, and insects. One of them, the little pol-pol, was at one time common in Port of Spain, where it used to catch insects under the electric lights.

Macaws of various colours and parrots are very pretty birds. Among them are the blue-headed parrot (*perruche à tête bleue*) and the seven-coloured parrot (*perruche à sept couleurs*).

HUMMING BIRD AND NEST.

The potoo or poor-me-one is an interesting night-bird. It sits on a stump and sings six mournful notes down the scale. For a long time people thought this song was sung by a mammal—the little anteater.

Trinidad is the "Land of the Humming Bird". There are fifteen kinds of this beautiful little creature, which flits about gathering insects from the flowers with its long beak. One of the best known is the emerald. It builds a neat tiny nest of fern leaves, seeds, spider's web, and cotton, made beautiful with green moss and lichen. Nineteen days after its two eggs are laid the young ones are hatched, and in three weeks more they are able to fly.

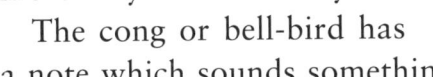

TOUCAN.

The cong or bell-bird has a note which sounds something very like a bell or an anvil. Its head is coffee-brown, its back and breast silver-grey, while its bill, wings, and feet are black. It also has a beard. The female is of a dull olive-green colour. Also, in Guyana there is another bell-bird which is white.

GROUND DOVE.

Doves, pigeons, cuckoos, woodpeckers, the keskidee (*qu'est-ce-qu'il-dit*), and the black boat-tail are also very common. The toucan, with its large yellow beak, is found in the forests on the Main, while in some islands a variety of this bird has a black and heliotrope beak. This is the one shown in the picture. Yellow-tails or corn-birds form their nests very cleverly hanging from the branches of trees.

NESTS OF YELLOW-TAIL OR CORN-BIRD.

Exercises

1. Write out the names of all these birds which you have seen. Give in another list the names of all those you have not seen. How many are there in each list?
2. Write out all the colours named in this lesson.
3. Draw a king corbeau, and colour it with crayons or pastels.
4. Fill in the blanks:
    (a) The —— is often seen on the backs of animals eating the ticks. It is a kind of cuckoo.
    (b) It is often thought that woodpeckers destroy cacao. They only eat —— which have got into the pods.
    (c) —— and —— are night-birds.
    (d) The —— is the smallest and the —— the largest bird named in this lesson.

LESSON 33

PICTURES AND STORIES

Do you like the stories in this book? I am sure that you do. A good story pleases everybody.

Ever since the world began, people have loved to tell stories and to hear them told. They have also loved to make pictures and to look at them.

A picture, such as the first one in this book, tells its own story. When we look at it we see things which make us think of a story. The story comes to us through what we may call the *eye-gate*.

If a man tells us a story, we listen to the words which he speaks. In this case the story comes to us through the *ear-gate*.

In olden days all stories were spoken and heard—that is, they all went in at the ear-gate. You learned in Book I. that these were called folk-tales. In some Eastern lands men still travel from place to place telling stories. In these lands

A TELLER OF TALES.
(*By Horace Vernet.*)

you may often see a crowd of people round a story-teller.

The painter uses colours; the storyteller uses words. There are two kinds of words—spoken words and written or printed words. Spoken words are made up of sounds which come to us through the ear-gate.

Written or printed words are made up of letters. Each letter stands for a sound, and it sends its message through the eye-gate.

Look at the printed word *Bad*. It is built up of three letters which stand for three different sounds. When we put these sounds together they make up the spoken word *Bad*.

Written or printed words come to us through the eye-gate. Yes, but they stand for sounds which come to us through the ear-gate.

In our country we do not often *hear* stories told. We *read* them. Our storyteller writes down his story in words. Then we can read the story for ourselves.

When the story is written we can do without the story-teller. He may be far away, or he may be dead. It does not matter. We have his story, and if we can read we can enjoy it anywhere and at any time.

Exercises

1. Answer the following questions in sentences:
   With what do you see?
   With what do you hear?
   With what do you smell?
   With what do you taste?
   With what do you feel?
2. Through which gate or gates do the following send their message: a picture, a story that is told, a song, velvet, perfume?
3. Suppose you had to lose either eye-gate or ear-gate, which would you choose to keep? Why?
4. Why do men write down their stories?
5. Which is your favourite story? Give reasons.
6. Write down the names of all the things you can see in the picture on page 150.
7. Which man is the "Teller of Tales" in the picture? How do you know?

READING TESTS AND EXERCISES

TEST I

Can you fill in the missing words in the following sentences?
1. Coal is black, but snow is very ——.
2. I am tall, but my brother is not. He is ——.
3. A ruler is long, but a pencil is not so long. It is ——.
4. We go to school in the daytime, but we sleep at ——.
5. The little flowers are low on the ground, but the stars are —— in the sky.
6. The floor is very hard, but my pillow is very —— under my head at night.
7. Our cat is fat, but the pup has been sick and he is not fat. He is ——.
8. My father's knife is so sharp that he will not let me use it. But my little knife is ——.
9. When we are happy we laugh, but when we feel sad we sometimes ——.

TEST II

The words in these sentences are badly mixed up Can you arrange them so as to make good sentences?
1. the in The horses are barn.
2. has legs The table four.
3. father away Did your go?
4. dirty is hand often Bobby's.

5. pail a girl The carries.
6. white clock has The a face.
7. pretty is Blue very chalk.
8. boys their Good work finish.
9. Mary the lamp light will.
10. see the I window through.
11. Will home now come you?
12. fruit Some trees have.
13. moon behind The a cloud is.
14. garden in Flowers the grow.

TEST III

Making an Index

Suppose some one asked you: "Is there anything about a monkey in this book?"

You would look through the book, with a pencil in your hand, and say, "Yes, on pages 58, 59, 62, 101, 102, 103, 104, 128, 129, 130, 131, 132, and 133."

Then you would write down:

> Monkey, 58, 59, 62, 101, 102, 103, 104, 128, 129, 130, 131, 132, 133.

Then suppose some one asked you: "Is there anything about a picture in this book?"

You would look through it again, and then write down:—

> Picture, 25, 27, 31, 36, 39, 71, 72, 74, 112, 125, 143, 149, 152.

Now find out in the same way the pages on which mention is made of the coconut, ship, rain, fruit, tree, ocean, water, king.

Make a line for each of the above, writing the word first and the numbers of the pages after it.

1. What are your initials? Write them down. What is the initial letter of hen, cock, sea, lamb?
2. Which letter comes first in the alphabet:
   h or *c*; *p* or *s*; *t* or *f*; *g* or *p*?
3. Arrange in their proper ABC order: *h, m,* and *b*; *p, q, a,* and *t*; *m, o, x,* and *c*; *z, f, g,* and *h*; *l, o, t,* and *y*.
4. Arrange in their proper ABC order, according to the initial letter: *Cow, ox, pig, sea, lamb,* and *man; fox, hen, chick, fairy,* and *bridge; curl, piper, door,* and *coat; window, cradle, bed,* and *hoop.*
5. Now arrange in the same way the names of things in this book with the numbers of the pages after them—for example:
    Coconut, — — — —
    Fruit, — — — —
    King, — — — —
    Monkey, — — — —
    Ocean, — — — —
    Picture, — — — —
    Rain, — — — —
    Ship, — — — —
    Tree, — — — —
    Water, — — — —
    (Supply page numbers as before.)

6. When you have done this you have made an INDEX of some of the things in this book. How could you use it?
7. Now write a list of the Pictures in this book in the order in which they are printed. Begin like this:

>CORN PLANT............ ... ...Page 8
>CHICKEN HAWK........ ... .Page 11

TEST IV

PICTURES

Words make us see pictures. Some are still or quiet pictures, others are moving pictures. Say whether each of the following pictures is still or moving:

(i) There's a ship on the sea,
And it's sailing to-night.
(ii) The lambs have now lain down to sleep.
(iii) Up into the cherry tree,
Who should climb but little me?
(iv) A sunshiny shower
Won't last half an hour.
(v) I wish I had a pretty house,
The smallest ever seen,
With funny little red walls,
And roof of mossy green.

TEST V

The Piper

(See coloured picture on page 159.)

1. What *persons* can you see in the picture? (Do not miss out any of them.)
2. What *things* can you see in the coloured picture?
3. Is the tall figure in the middle of the picture a man or a woman? How do you know?
4. If he is playing a *pipe,* what shall we call him?
5. Read and learn these lines:
    "His queer long coat from heel to head,
    Was half of yellow and half of red,
    And he himself was tall and thin,
    With sharp blue eyes, each like a pin;
    And light, loose hair, yet swarthy skin,
    No tuft on cheek, nor beard on chin,
    But lips where smiles went out and in."
6. Which half of the coat was yellow, and which half was red?
7. Do you think the artist has made his eyes "each like a pin"?
8. Has the artist given the Piper a "swarthy skin"?
9. Read and learn these lines:
    "To blow the pipe his lips he wrinkled,
    And green and blue his sharp eyes twinkled,
    Like a candle-flame where salt is sprinkled."
10. When you get home ask your mother to let you find out whether the last line is true.

11. Read and learn these lines:

> "Like fowls in a farmyard when barley is scattering,
> Out come the children running.
> All the little boys and girls,
> With rosy cheeks and flaxen curls,
> And sparkling eyes and teeth like pearls,
> Tripping and skipping, ran merrily after
> The wonderful music with shouting and laughter.
>
> *   *   *   *   *
>
> And the Piper advanced and the children followed,
> And when all were in to the very last,
> The door in the mountain-side shut fast."

12. Are the people on the pavement sorry or glad to see the children follow the Piper? Do you think they could stop them? If not, why not?

13. Can you count the number of children?

14. What is the music doing to their feet?

15. Why is one of the houses in the coloured picture made only as big as the Piper's body?

16. Here is a nearer view of one of the men at the side of the picture. What do you think he is saying?

THE PIPER.

TEST VI

THE HINDU AND THE CHINA JAR

A Hindu had a large blue china jar which was worth a great deal of money, but which might be very easily broken.

So he made a silver cord, which he passed round the neck of the jar and then finished it off in a loop.

By this loop he hung the jar on a peg in the wall just above his couch.

One day he had some butter and honey left over from his midday meal; so he put it into the blue china jar.

Then he leant back on his couch with a stick in his hand and began to think aloud.

"Butter and honey are very dear," he said, "and the price is likely to rise higher and still higher.

"I will save a little each day and put it into this blue china jar. When the jar is full, I will sell it at a very high price, and will buy ten goats with the money.

"In two years the ten goats will be four hundred. These shall be sold and the money spent on a small herd of cattle.

"In a few years more the small herd will be a large one, and I shall make much profit and be a very wealthy man.

"Then I will marry and have a son who will be the heir to all my riches.

"If he obeys me, all will be well. But if he does not obey me, I will——"

He raised the stick as if to strike his son, who was not there, and struck the blue china jar, which fell in pieces at his feet.

Exercises

1. Would the Hindu wear a tall silk hat and a black coat? If not, what would he wear?
2. In which country did he live?
3. Which of these words can be used to describe the Hindu?—

    kind, cruel, wise, foolish, greedy, careful, careless, good-tempered.
4. Where does honey come from?
5. Which is busier, a cow or a bee? Which is cleverer? Why?
6. If you could paint a picture to go with this story, what would you show in it?

TEST VII

THE MAID AND THE PAIL OF MILK

A MAID milked a cow and got a large wooden pail full of fresh milk. She put a pad on her head, placed the pail on the pad, and set out across the fields for her master's dairy.

As she stepped carefully across the grass she talked to herself.

"Master said I might keep this milk for myself.

"I will take the cream from it and make it into butter. On Saturday I will take my butter to the market and sell it for a good price.

"With the money I get for the butter I will buy two chickens, which will soon lay a large number of eggs. I will sell these eggs at the market; and in a few months I shall have a nice little store of money.

"As soon as I have saved enough money I will buy a cow. The cow will have a calf, which will bring a high price in the market. I will also make butter and cheese from the milk, and get still more money, with which I will buy more cows. In time I shall become very rich. Then I shall have many sweethearts.

"But I shall be in no hurry to choose a husband. I will dress in fine silks and laces, and will toss my head at all of them—like this!"

As she tossed her head, the pail toppled over, and the milk was all spilt upon the ground.

Exercises

1. Why did the milkmaid put a pad upon her head?
2. Why did she walk so carefully across the grass?
3. Have you ever seen a market? If so, tell what can be seen there.
4. Make a list of twelve things which may be sold at a market.
5. Why was the maid going to toss her head at her sweethearts?
6. If you could paint a picture to go at the end of this story, what would you show in it?
7. Try to make a rough sketch of this picture as you would like it to be.
8. In what way or ways are the last two stories like each other?

9. Which of the following words can be used to describe the Hindu and can also be used to describe the milkmaid?—

   proud, selfish, cruel, silly, clever, pretty, greedy, wise.
10. Try to make up another story like the last two stories. There is one told about an Arab who sold fine glass-ware which stood on a tray in the market-place near his feet. Perhaps you can think it out for yourself.

ADDITIONAL POETRY FOR READING AND RECITATION

Day

"I am busy," said the sea.
"I am busy. Think of me.
Making continents to be.
I am busy," said the sea.

"I am busy," said the rain.
"When I fall, it's not in vain;
Wait and you will see the grain.
I am busy," said the rain.

"I am busy," said the air,
"Blowing here and blowing there,
Up and down and everywhere.
I am busy," said the air.

"I am busy," said the sun.
"All my planets, every one,
Know my work is never done.
I am busy," said the sun.

Sea and rain and air and sun,
Here's a fellow toiler:—one
Whose task will soon be done.

Sir Cecil Spring Rice.
(*By permission of Lady Spring Rice.*)

Piping Down the Valleys

Piping down the valleys wild,
   Piping songs of pleasant glee,
On a cloud I saw a child,
   And he, laughing, said to me:

"Pipe a song about a lamb,"
   So I piped with merry cheer;
"Piper, pipe that song again."
   So I piped—he wept to hear.

"Drop thy pipe, thy happy pipe,
   Sing thy songs of happy cheer;"
So I sung the same again,
   While he wept with joy to hear.

"Piper, sit thee down and write
   In a book, that all may read."
So he vanished from my sight;
   And I plucked a hollow reed.

And I made a rural pen,
   And I stained the water clear,
And I wrote my happy songs,
   Every child may joy to hear.

WILLIAM BLAKE.

LITTLE GIRLS

IF no one ever marries me,—
   And I don't see why they should
For nurse says I'm not pretty,
   And I'm seldom very good—

If no one ever marries me
   I shan't mind very much,
I shall buy a squirrel in a cage,
   And a little rabbit-hutch;

I shall have a cottage near a wood,
   And a pony all my own,
And a little lamb, quite clean and tame,
   That I can take to town;

And when I'm getting really old,—
   At twenty eight or nine—
I shall buy a little orphan girl
   And bring her up as mine.
                  LAURENCE ALMA TADEMA.
                (By permission of the Author.)

MY KINGDOM

DOWN by a shining water well
I found a very little dell,
   No higher than my head.

The heather and the gorse about
In summer bloom were coming out,
   Some yellow and some red.

I called the little pool a sea;
The little hills were big to me;
   For I am very small.
I made a boat, I made a town,
I searched the caverns up and down
   And named them one and all.

And all about was mine, I said,
The little sparrows overhead,
   The little minnows too.
This was the world, and I was king;
For me the bees came by to sing,
   For me the swallows flew.

I played there were no deeper seas,
Nor any wider plains than these,
   Nor other kings than me.
At last I heard my mother call
Out from the house at evenfall,
   To call me home to tea.

And I must rise and leave my dell,
And leave my dimpled water well,
  And leave my heather blooms.
Alas! and as my home I neared,
How very big my nurse appeared,
  How great and cool the rooms!
From "A Child's Garden of Verses" by
Robert Louis Stevenson.
*(By permission of
Messrs. Longmans, Green, and Co., Ltd.)*

The Spider and the Fly

"Will you walk into my parlour?" said the Spider to the Fly,—
"Tis the prettiest little parlour that ever you did spy;
The way into my parlour is up a winding stair,
And I have many curious things to show when you are there."
"Oh no, no," said the little Fly, "to ask me is in vain,
For who goes up your winding stair can ne'er come down again."

"I'm sure you must be weary, dear, with soaring up so high;

Will you rest upon my little bed?" said the Spider to the Fly.
"There are pretty curtains drawn around, the sheets are fine and thin,
And if you like to rest a while, I'll snugly tuck you in!"
"Oh no, no," said the little Fly, "for I've often heard it said,
They never, never wake again, who sleep upon your bed!"

Said the cunning Spider to the Fly: "Dear friend, what can I do
To prove the warm affection I've always felt for you?
I have, within my pantry, good store of all that's nice;
I'm sure you're very welcome—will you please to take a slice?"
"Oh no, no," said the little Fly, "kind sir, that cannot be,
I've heard what's in your pantry, and I do not wish to see!"

"Sweet creature," said the Spider, "you're witty and you're wise;

How handsome are your gauzy wings, how
  brilliant are your eyes!
I have a little looking-glass upon my parlour
  shelf,
If you'll step in one moment, dear, you shall
  behold yourself."
"I thank you, gentle sir," she said, "for what
  you're pleased to say,
And bidding you good-morning now, I'll call
  another day."

The Spider turned him round about, and went
  into his den,
For well he knew the silly Fly would soon come
  back again;
So he wove a subtle web, in a little corner sly,
And set his table ready, to dine upon the Fly.
Then he came out to his door again, and merrily
  did sing,—
"Come hither, hither, pretty Fly, with the pearl
  and silver wing;
Your robes are green and purple, there's a crest
  upon your head;
Your eyes are like the diamond bright, but mine
  are dull as lead!"

Alas, alas! how very soon this silly little Fly,
Hearing his wily, flattering words, came slowly flitting by:
With buzzing wings she hung aloft, then near and nearer drew,—
Thinking only of her brilliant eyes, and green and purple hue,
Thinking only of her crested head—poor foolish thing! At last,
Up jumped the cunning Spider, and fiercely held her fast;
He dragged her up his winding stair, into his dismal den,
Within his little parlour—but she ne'er came out again!

And now, dear little children who may this story read,
To idle, silly, flattering words, I pray you, ne'er give heed:
Unto an evil counsellor close heart, and ear, and eye,
And take a lesson from this tale of the Spider and the Fly.

MARY HOWITT.

Some One

Some one came knocking
   At my wee, small door;
Some one came knocking,
   I'm sure—sure—sure;
I listened, I opened,
   I looked to left and right,
But nought there was a-stirring
   In the still dark night;
Only the busy beetle
   Tap-tapping in the wall,
Only from the forest
   The screech-owl's call,
Only the cricket whistling
   While the dewdrops fall—
So I know not who came knocking,
   At all, at all, at all.

WALTER DE LA MARE.
(By permission of the Author.)

Dirty Jim

There was one little Jim;
   'Tis reported of him—
And 'tis to his lasting disgrace—

That he never was seen
With his hands at all clean,
Nor yet ever clean was his face.

His friends were much hurt
To see so much dirt,
And often they made him quite clean;
But all was in vain—
He was dirty again,
And never was fit to be seen.

It gave him no pain
To hear them complain,
Nor his own dirty clothes to survey;
His indolent mind
No pleasure could find
In tidy and wholesome array.

The idle and bad,
Like this little lad,
May love dirty ways, to be sure;
But good boys are seen
To be decent and clean,
Although they are ever so poor.

T. L. Peacock.

What Became of Them?

He was a rat, and she was a rat,
   And down in one hole they did dwell,
And both were as black as a witch's cat,
   And they loved one another well.

He had a tail, and she had a tail,
   Both long and curling and fine;
And each said, "Yours is the finest tail
   In the world, excepting mine."

He smelt the cheese, and she smelt the cheese,
   And they both pronounced it good;
And both remarked it would greatly add
   To the charms of their daily food.

So he ventured out, and she ventured out,
   And I saw them go with pain;
But what befell them I never can tell,
   For they never came back again.

Song

Sweet and low, sweet and low,
Wind of the western sea,
Low, low, breathe and blow,
Wind of the western sea!
Over the rolling waters go,
Come from the dying moon, and blow,
Blow him again to me;
While my little one, while my pretty one sleeps.

Sleep and rest, sleep and rest,
Father will come to thee soon;
Rest, rest, on mother's breast,
Father will come to thee soon;
Father will come to his babe in the nest,
Silver sails all out of the west
Under the silver moon:
Sleep, my little one, sleep, my pretty one, sleep.

Tennyson.
(*From "The Princess"*)